THE BOOK OF
CANDLES

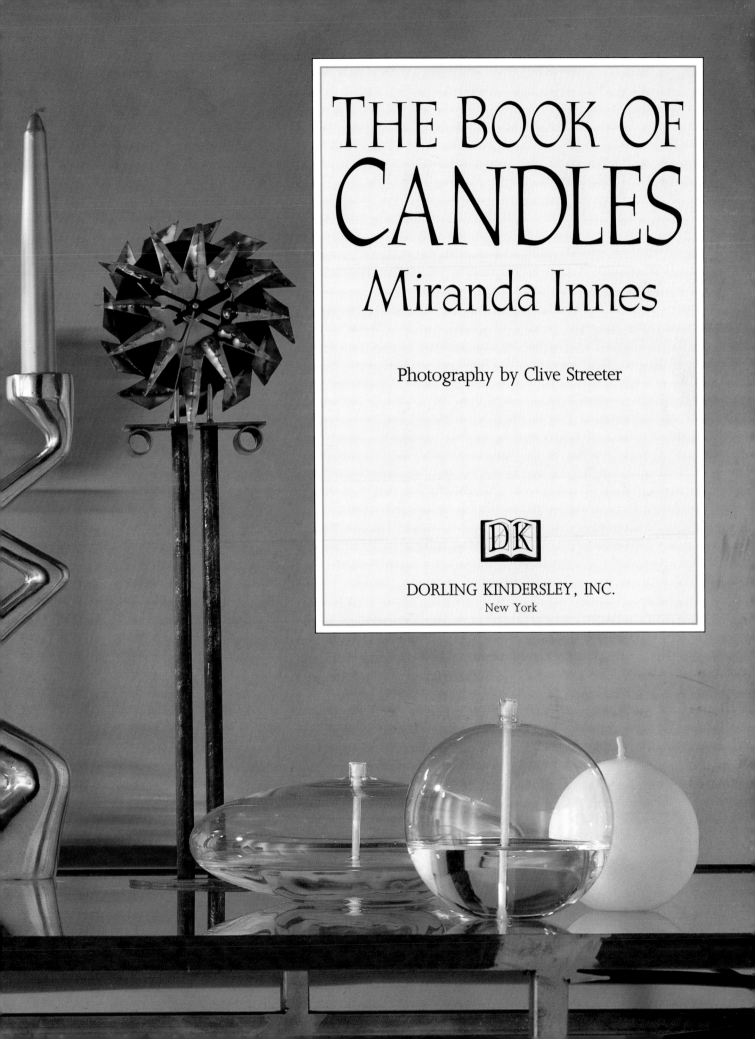

THE BOOK OF
CANDLES
Miranda Innes

Photography by Clive Streeter

DK

DORLING KINDERSLEY, INC.
New York

To Will, Leo, and Roger

A DORLING KINDERSLEY BOOK

Art Editor Sarah Scrutton
Project Editor Claire Le Bas

Art Director Anne-Marie Bulat
Managing Editor Daphne Razazan

Production Controller Deborah Wehner

First American Edition, 1991
1 3 5 7 9 10 8 6 4 2
Dorling Kindersley, Inc., 232 Madison
Avenue, New York, New York 10016

ISBN 1-879431-05-X
Library of Congress Catalog Card Number
91-060146

Reproduced by J. Film, Singapore
Printed and bound by Cayfosa Industria
Grafica, Barcelona

CONTENTS

Introduction 6

A CATALOG OF
CANDLES & CANDLESTICKS

DECORATING WITH CANDLES

THE ART OF MAKING CANDLES

INTRODUCTION

Music-making
Players perform by
candlelight in
The Concert by
Hendrick ter Brugghen.

C andles create instant atmosphere—their glow makes an intimate and comforting sphere, with a touch of romance and a sense of warmth. There is something about the flickering golden flame that transforms a humble supper into *dîner à deux*—the enchanted circle of light encourages people to look at each other anew, to appreciate and listen with long-forgotten fascination.

Until the convenient, but somewhat less romantic, virtues of kerosene and gas were discovered, it was by candlelight that books were written, songs sung, passions kindled, and weddings celebrated. Julius Caesar made plans by candlelight, Dante worshiped Beatrice, Shakespeare pondered his Dark Lady, Caravaggio painted Bacchus. Churches exhaled the sweet smell of beeswax, and the streets of Pepys's London were rank with the stench of tallow candles.

A powerful focus
The bright, steady flame has an almost hypnotic effect in this painting of *Christ before the High Priest* by Gerrit van Honthorst.

The little flame was the emblem of hope, life, truth, virtue, wisdom, and in religious observance, of the love of God. At Candlemas, all the candles to be used in the church in the coming year are blessed, in remembrance of the presentation of Jesus in the temple, when the aged Simeon addressed Christ as the Light of the World.

Rushlights and the much reviled tallow candles were the only recourse of the poor until the 19th century. The slaughter of one bull provided enough tallow for three years' worth of candles, and a well-organized household would produce 300 or so in a candle-making session. In 13th-century Paris, the members of a guild of tallow chandlers went from house to house making candles. In the 15th century, a candlemaker named de Brez, of Paris, revolutionized the business by inventing the candle mold. Beeswax resisted the newfangled mold, and until this century, with the discovery of silicon releasing agents, it has always been shaped by dipping. In France and Britain, the Guild of Wax Chandlers was created to protect beeswax workers from taint by association with tallow-chandlers.

In a particularly punitive piece of British legislation, candles were taxed in 1709, and people were forbidden to make their own. This progressively more stringent tax was finally repealed in 1831, resulting in a renaissance of decorative candles. But it was not until almost too

Street market
Candlelight casts a glow over the wares in *The Gamestall* by Petras van Schendel.

late, when more convenient alternatives were on the horizon, that a Frenchman called Chevreul purified tallow by treating it with alkali and sulphuric acid, producing the clean-burning, long-lasting stearin candle.

Another Frenchman, named Cambaceres, came up with the braided wick in 1825, which he pickled in mineral salts to make it curve during burning, thus obviating all the fussy necessities of wick trimming and the familiar unpleasantness of smoke. Joseph Morgan created a candle-making machine in 1834 that could turn out 1,500 candles an hour, and two years later, a palm oil substance, palmatine, was patented as an alternative to existing waxes. In the mid-19th century, candle-making companies owned coconut palm plantations in Sri Lanka and could produce a hundred tons of candles weekly. In 1850, paraffin wax appeared, and in 1857, in combination with stearin and the braided wick, it finally resulted in bright, affordable candles. This precisely coincided with the sudden availability of inexpensive kerosene lamps: the candle was eclipsed.

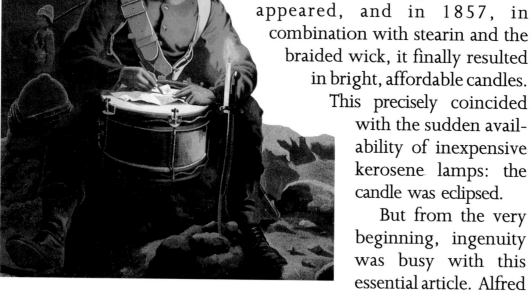

Making candles
Molten wax was scooped up from the vat and poured over the suspended wicks until they were the desired diameter.

But from the very beginning, ingenuity was busy with this essential article. Alfred

Letter to a loved one
From an early advertisement, *Soldier Boy*, for Price's Candles.

the Great devised an answer to the all too easily extinguished flame, consisting of a thin shield of horn to protect it against drafts. A thousand years ago, the candle clock was invented, which marked the hours, somewhat inaccurately, by burning a candle with 12 horizontal lines painted on its side. In 17th-century England, bidding at an auction was conducted to the light of an inch-high candle—when it guttered out, bidding closed.

These days, barring power outages, candles have no other function than to give pleasure and to provide a nostalgic alternative light source. The smooth glossiness of machine-made candles, the fragrance of beeswax, the sweetness of scented candles make them lovely objects in themselves. They are the cheapest piece of theater—a couple of red candles and a pine branch make an instant

Romantic lanterns
Lighting paper lanterns with tapers in *Carnation, Lily, Lily, Rose* by John Singer Sargent.

Christmas; a bouquet of white roses with sugar-pink candles creates romantic seclusion; tall wrought iron candlesticks holding beeswax cylinders have the swashbuckling bravado of the Three Musketeers. It is surprising what you can do with wax and string.

A CATALOG
OF CANDLES &
CANDLESTICKS

From the simplest and most
utilitarian candles with their plain
intrinsic beauty, to the glittering
prisms of the most sophisticated
and intricately wrought
candelabra, this is a source book
for the essential elements of
candle power, illustrating the
great diversity of colors and
shapes, decoration and finishes
available, offering inspiration for
making your own candles at
home plus an indispensable
buyer's guide.

Dipped candles

The oldest method of candle-making, dipping involves repeatedly immersing a wick in molten wax until enough layers accumulate to form a candle of the desired width. The technique has been used since Roman times, when a slim roll of papyrus was dipped into beeswax bleached by the sun. Dipped candles usually come in pairs; cut crosswise they display concentric rings of wax like the rings on a tree trunk. The candles have a tapered shape and uneven bases. A loop of wick between the pair makes a handle for dipping into the vat of molten wax.

Wick forming
a handle for
dipping

Traditional dipped
Old-fashioned elegance combines with an odorless, clean flame in these candles made of paraffin wax.

6¹/₂ in
(16.5cm) pair

8 in
(20cm) pair

12 in
(30cm) pair

Basic color

First dip   Second dip   Final dip

Striped candles

Achieved by overdipping candles in several different colors, taking in less of their length at each dip, such striped candles—often in rainbow hues—have a note of rustic hippydom.

Tallow candles

Made of wax extracted from the fat of cattle and sheep, tallow produces acrid candles that obscure almost as much light with smoke as they shed with flame. For centuries they were the main form of artificial lighting for the poor. In 1661, John Evelyn complained of " those horrid stinks, nidorous and unwhole-some smells which proceed from tallow."

Drip at the base is formed by the molten wax running down

Church candles

The unself-conscious legacy of ancient tradition, church candles have survived almost unchanged for centuries. Symbolizing purity, life, the soul, the unquenchable light of faith, and the love of God for man, they are an essential element in religious ceremonies throughout the world. Traditionally made with a high proportion of beeswax, church candles are available from many candle shops and have a classic simplicity that looks good in any setting.

Processional tapers

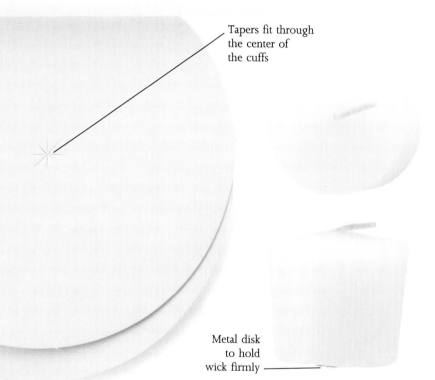

Tapers fit through the center of the cuffs

Metal disk to hold wick firmly

Tapers and cuffs
Paper cuffs around slender processional tapers prevent dripping wax from burning the hands of those holding them.

18 in (45cm) altar candle

Votum candles
Placed in a side-chapel in a red or blue glass container, these burn constantly and slowly in remembrance of the dead.

Votive candles
These are lit by the laity to solemnize a prayer and burn in serried ranks on stands consisting of 21 or 36 prickets.

9 in (23cm)
altar candle

6¹/₂ in (16.5cm)
altar candle

6¹/₂ in (16.5cm)
septalite

6in (15cm)
altar
candle

Altar candles (above and below)
Varying in height from six inches to almost three feet, these stand in magnificent candlesticks flanking the altar and are lit for the duration of a service.

Septalite (above)
A very grand and somewhat more convenient votum light than the little side-chapel versions, septalites burn for a full seven days.

8 in (20cm)
altar candle

Beeswax candles

Simplest and best, beeswax candles are the most precious, burning slowly and clearly with a wonderful honey fragrance. Beeswax is difficult to mold, and the classic production method involves dipping—an expensive and time-consuming business. Producing honeycomb is labor-intensive for the bees too, so nowadays beekeepers give them a head start by providing a ready-made base for the wax honeycomb.

Dipped beeswax
The classic tapered cylinder.

Molded beeswax
Wax can be molded into any shape, but simplicity best suits the qualities of beeswax.

Molded beehive—a clever visual pun

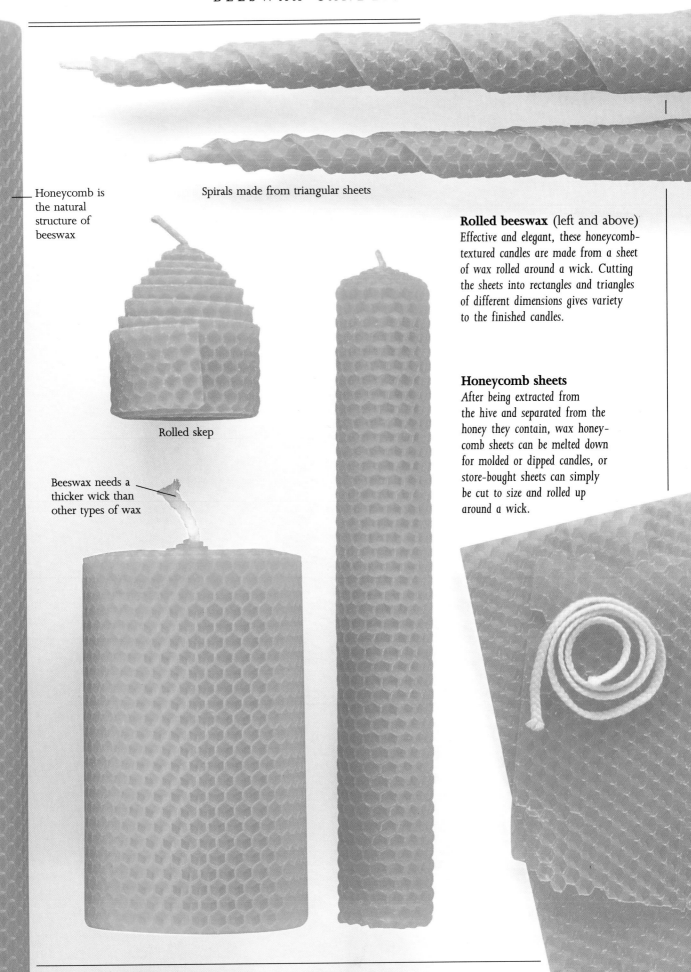

Honeycomb is the natural structure of beeswax

Spirals made from triangular sheets

Rolled skep

Beeswax needs a thicker wick than other types of wax

Rolled beeswax (left and above)
Effective and elegant, these honeycomb-textured candles are made from a sheet of wax rolled around a wick. Cutting the sheets into rectangles and triangles of different dimensions gives variety to the finished candles.

Honeycomb sheets
After being extracted from the hive and separated from the honey they contain, wax honeycomb sheets can be melted down for molded or dipped candles, or store-bought sheets can simply be cut to size and rolled up around a wick.

Christmas candles

There is a natural affinity between candles and Christmas time, which goes back to pagan midwinter solar observances: the turning point of the year at its darkest nadir celebrated defiantly with lights and evergreens. From the north and Celtic culture came yuletide expressed in the candle-decked Christmas tree, later popularized by Prince Albert; and, with a Christian mixture of symbolic fires and lights, we end up with the unbeatable classic combination of glowing red, green, and gold candles.

Molded candle overdipped in gold

Plasticized glaze for a shiny finish

Advent candle
The twenty-four holy days of Advent are marked by burning one section each day.

Decorated candles
Every aspect of Christmas finds exuberant expression in wax trees, angels, St. Nicholas, the star of Bethlehem.

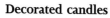

Molded tassel

Applied glitter

Painted colors

Tree candle (right)
For a traditional touch, decorate the tree with candles; attach them securely in clip-on holders, and never leave them unattended.

Molded star

Classic spiral

Gold thread spiral

Snow-flake of applied wax

Molded column

Holly leaf transfer

Ribbon of applied wax

A rainbow of lights

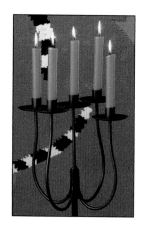

Lit or unlit, candles are pure, clear color, available in a spectrum of harmonizing shades that are a decorator's dream—they echo and reflect any kind of interior design. They look wonderful grouped, with families of colors side by side. Subtle partnerships can be made with candlesticks: use rich, warm colors dappled with gold to reflect the opulence of a gilded baroque candlestick, or steely gray to give a metallic echo to pewter. Candles are the inexpensive, replaceable equivalent of fashion accessories, and the colors are there to be enjoyed—tall fondant pink tapers, cool Scandinavian blues and greens, glowing fiery reds and yellows.

Blues and greens
Sky and sea, leaves and spring flowers—these are the colors of nature, equally at home with both pale rustic wood and the milky blue droplets of Venetian glass candelabra.

Creams and yellows
Celebrate spring with candles in fresh, sunny colors surrounded by terra-cotta pots of primroses.

Pinks
Sunrise, apple blossoms, cotton candy— pink is the color of innocence and youth, particularly in combination with white daisies and other flowers.

Reds
Shining strawberries, glittering garnets and rubies, fire and flame—reds signify warmth and passion, richness and luxury, and create an instant festive look.

Candle shapes

As anyone who has been unable to resist fiddling with melting wax knows, part of the allure of candles is their sculptural quality. Molded, carved, or twisted, they can have the flawless smooth translucence of jade or the rugged textured corrugations of a piece of farm equipment. Perfect spheres or intricate carved spirals, Santa Claus or shiny red hearts for Valentine's Day, dark matte geometric shapes to cluster on a black lacquer tray in a stark modern interior, elegant spirals to grace antique silver candelabra— there are shapes to match every whim, every style of decoration.

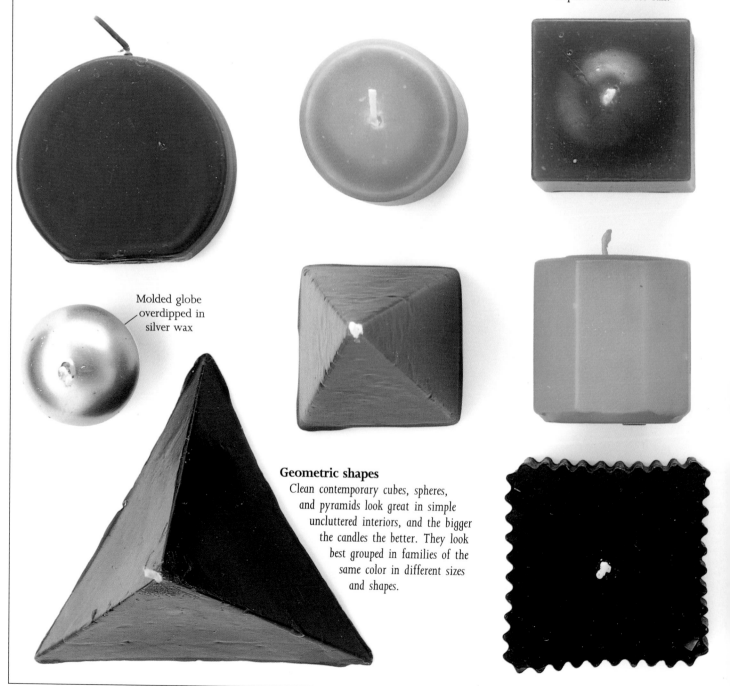

Representational shapes
The lighter side of candle design— disposable kitsch for fun.

Molded globe overdipped in silver wax

Geometric shapes
Clean contemporary cubes, spheres, and pyramids look great in simple uncluttered interiors, and the bigger the candles the better. They look best grouped in families of the same color in different sizes and shapes.

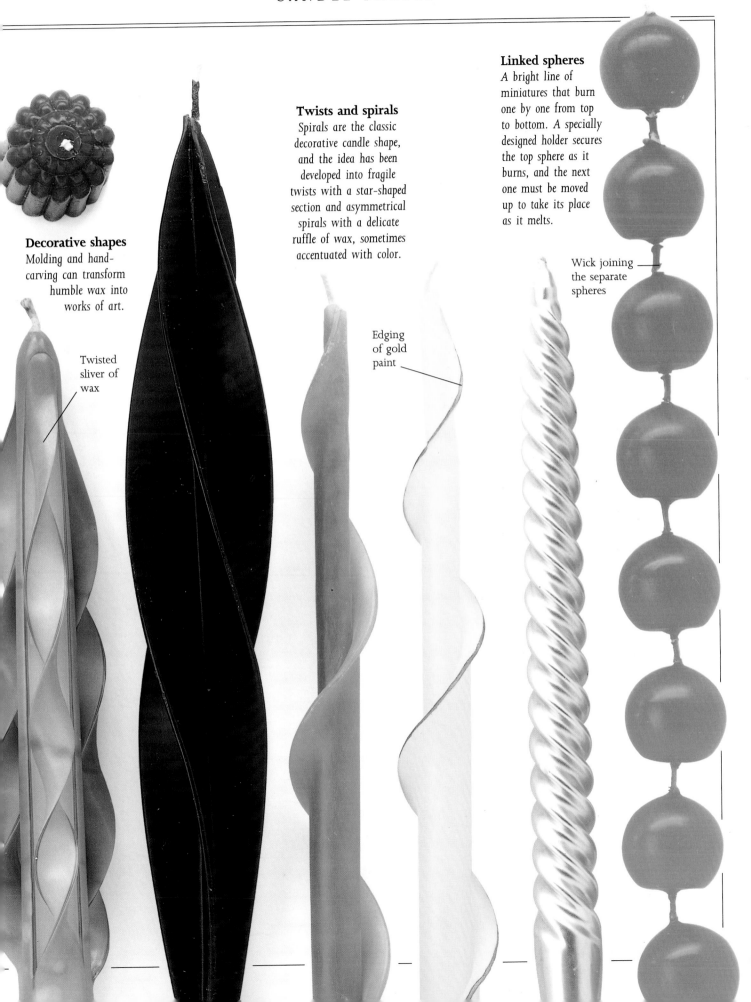

Linked spheres

A bright line of miniatures that burn one by one from top to bottom. A specially designed holder secures the top sphere as it burns, and the next one must be moved up to take its place as it melts.

Wick joining the separate spheres

Twists and spirals

Spirals are the classic decorative candle shape, and the idea has been developed into fragile twists with a star-shaped section and asymmetrical spirals with a delicate ruffle of wax, sometimes accentuated with color.

Edging of gold paint

Decorative shapes

Molding and hand-carving can transform humble wax into works of art.

Twisted sliver of wax

Decorated candles

There are no hard and fast rules for choosing decorated candles—the only guide is what you like and what suits the context. Find candles to complement your possessions—a bold painted design echoes bright Provençal pottery, the fragile charm of pressed flower candles matches delicate Victorian porcelain, and the sumptuous richness of stippled and gilded candles looks beautiful in an Art Nouveau setting.

Mottled finish (right)
A professional finish with a fine lacy veil of white wax over color.

Simple hand-painted design

Marbled and streaked
Subtle swirls of blue and green are achieved by floating different colored waxes on a dipping bath and immersing the candle briefly.

Sponged colors

Stenciled decoration

Paint finishes
Hand-painting has a naive charm, at home with peasant crockery. Sponged, stenciled, and stippled candles vary from the bold to the sophisticated.

Stippled candle

Small flowers and leaves make pretty decorations

Carved patterns

Pressed flowers
Endowed with old-fashioned charm, these candles are perfect as presents.

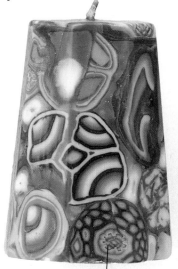

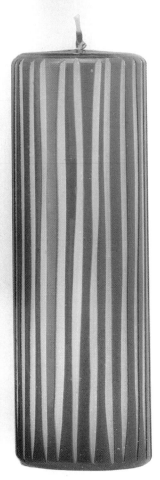

A bright mosaic of rolled and cut wax

Applied wax
Tiny pieces of wax can be attached to a candle with wax glue. Surface decoration can be as varied as the imagination can concoct— from a sprinkling of colored flecks to a delicate spiral of twisted strands.

Multicolored
Covered with lozenges cut from rolls of wax overdipped in bright colors, these candles glow like stained glass when lit.

Carved decorations
Candles with an outer coating of strong color are carved to reveal the white wax beneath. These candles burn with a latticelike effect through the dark exterior.

Scented and floating candles

B esides shedding a warm and flattering light, candles can also fill a room with fragrance—even unscented candles burn away noxious smells, and outdoors, citronella will keep mosquitoes at a distance. The addition of perfume oil to a candle makes the wax more liquid, so most scented candles come in containers; if they are freestanding, they should be burned in a glass that will hold the melted wax. There is a huge choice of fragrances, some fresh and floral, some musky and oriental. What appeals to you is bound to be a personal matter—but choosing scented candles is one of life's more agreeable problems. Floating candles are often scented —their broad shapes and the cool water prevent the molten wax from spreading into a puddle.

Refillable silver container

Freestanding candles
Made in a spectrum of colors, these look pretty in groups in pressed glass containers.

Candles in containers
The subtle richness of high-quality candles is enhanced by elegant containers of silver, glass, or terra-cotta.

Dried flowers
Simple scented candles look good in plain terra-cotta or sand-colored holders with a drift of dried flowers or potpourri.

Floating candles
A flotilla of stars and flowers, their dancing lights reflected in water and on glass—floating candles are as hypnotic as firelight and as romantic as Mediterranean harbor lights on a phosphorescent sea.

Float rose petals among the candles

Displaying the candles
Reflective bowls of faceted glass or metal make the most of floating-candle flames. The water can be delicately tinted with food coloring or sprinkled with small flowers, petals, or even sequins. For safety, use a broad-based bowl with an outcurving lip.

Garden candles

Lanterns, lamps, outdoor torches, or terra-cotta pots filled with wax—candlelight is the most evocative garden lighting, but it does require a little care and a generous supply of matches. In the Orient, paper lanterns are used to shield the flame from wind, and during the Catholic fiesta in Santa Fe, the streets are filled with celebrants bearing candles in cups. At home, pathways and steps can be marked beautifully by standing a candle in sand in a small paper bag. For dining alfresco, a collection of night-lights in glasses or jars and a storm lamp or two are the most breeze-resistant lighting, and lanterns look pretty hung from trees—but pay attention to any overhanging branches.

Lanterns
Oriental pierced tin and brass lanterns make candle flames twinkle like starlight. More common is the utilitarian variety, often consisting of a metal frame with transparent or transluscent panels.

Flowerpot candles
These burn slowly, and the multiple wicks are strong enough to withstand a breeze. They are simple to make at home and the candles even look good in an old hand-made pot.

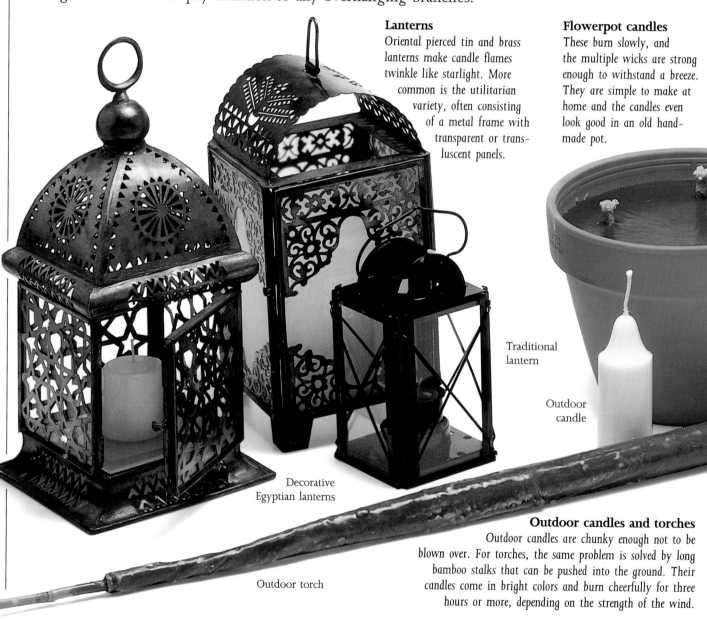

Traditional lantern

Outdoor candle

Decorative Egyptian lanterns

Outdoor torch

Outdoor candles and torches
Outdoor candles are chunky enough not to be blown over. For torches, the same problem is solved by long bamboo stalks that can be pushed into the ground. Their candles come in bright colors and burn cheerfully for three hours or more, depending on the strength of the wind.

28

Candle lamps

A cluster of candle lamps makes a sparkling centerpiece on a dinner table. The flame is protected from a breeze by a globe or bowl of clear, etched, or colored glass, much like the shade on oil lamps for which these candle holders were the forerunner. There are hanging versions, too —bell shapes in clear or colored glass.

The glass bowl can be lifted off the base

Storm lantern with metal base for stability

Egyptian storm lantern

Metal candlesticks

The classic material for candlesticks, metal can be worked into virtually any shape, from delicate filigree flowers to robust pillars. Antique metal candlesticks tend to survive longer than their more fragile ceramic and glass counterparts, gaining character with centuries of polishing and the occasional dent. The 18th century was the peak of candle power: elegant ormolu and silver candlesticks survive in large numbers. Today, nostalgia for the lively warmth of candlelight has started a renaissance of the old designs, from Gothic wrought iron to traditional pewter. At the same time experimentation with new methods and materials has introduced some entirely original ideas.

Traditional candlesticks
Contemporary wrought iron and brass with prickets and cups, or built-in snuffers, pay homage to the grace and simplicity of ancient designs. Irregularity is part of the charm. They are at home in cottage or condominium.

Classic style
Stately interpretations of antique designs in silver, gilt, brass, and bronze are perfect with antique furniture.

Country-style pewter

Floral silver-plate candlestick

Modern reproduction of traditional design

Classic silver candlestick

An unusual combination of ceramic and silver

Gilt animals and mythical figures are typical of the 18th century

Baroque outburst in the form of an exuberant silver frog

Chamber candle-stick with built-in snuffer

Tin holder with attached match-box container

Modern designs

Candlesticks range from a victory wreath with a glass lens to magnify the candle flame, to a shiny brass and copper sunflower intended to be clamped to the bath and hold a soothing nightcap. Wire, verdigris, and iron can manifest simple charm or sophisticated wit, following sinuous contortions or utter rectitude.

Verdigris finish

Classical wreath combining copper, iron, and glass

Glass lens

Traditional twisted iron candlestick

The malleability of copper allows functional eccentricity

Clock candlestick —a modern variation on the ancient candle timer

Sculptural form in plastic and bronze

Clamp to attach holder to the bath

Candlestick of bent and twisted wire

Distressed copper holder

Ceramic candlesticks

I ntricately patterned and delicately colored candlesticks are a natural extension of the richness of our ceramic heritage—there are echoes of the Orient, of South America, India, and the Mediterranean, there are unpredictable shiny glazes and demure Victorian sprigged transfers, hand-painted patterns and plain matte terra-cotta. Simple columnar designs withstand the firing process best, and a carefully controlled element of irregularity adds an eccentric charm to hand-crafted candlesticks. Few antiques remain (most of the survivors come from 19th-century dresser sets) but there is an avalanche of brightly decorated contemporary imports.

Designer

Quirky, quaint, definitely unique, these are love or hate candlesticks. They are surprisingly adaptable, and look good in both country cottages and stark architectural surroundings.

Ethnic

With no pretensions to being fine art, fluent hand-painting blended with strange and wonderful local traditions—an elephants' head base, for example —gives these candlesticks personality. The best setting is one that highlights their color or provides a suitable ethnic context.

Antique
elephant candlestick
from China

Thai blue and
white ware

Naive pottery
from Portugal

Organic shapes by
contemporary designers

Bold surface decoration

Spongeware
An ancient method of transferring designs to ceramics, spongeware has a robust and rustic simplicity. Once, the patterns were printed with pieces of potato, and the method used on modern spongeware is not much more sophisticated.

Floral
Pretty, delicate, and very feminine, dressing-table candlesticks in tasteful florals look best in a bedroom, adorning a bed-side table or mantelpiece.

Classic columns
Restrained colors and an unadorned, dignified shape—these are candlesticks that look good in any context and are an affordable pastiche of antique silver.

Floral transfer

Fruit and flowers—typical spongeware themes

Molded garland decoration

Square plinths echo 19th-century styles

33

Glass candlesticks

From the simplest column to the most ornate confection of twists and rainbow droplets, the transparency and sparkle of glass make it a natural partner to candlelight. A single handsome frosted glass candlestick looks good, but a whole crowd of rich rose-window colors and prismatic facets looks stunning. Classics are deeply cut crystal, glittering dark Bohemian glass, elaborately decorated Venetian glass from Murano, swirling opalescent Art Nouveau—or more affordable, though highly decorative, Victorian pressed glass.

Handcrafted

Glass is all things to all men: a liquid when molten and brittle when hard, it lends itself to both sinuous twists and glinting shards.

Squares of glass stacked into glittering ziggurats

Blown glass

Colored glass

Glass is the perfect medium for color: both subtle and rich tones glow with pure intensity. Make the most of colored glass by grouping candlesticks together so that the light shines through them.

The ornate patterning was intended to disguise the seam on molded glass

Molded glass

Press-molding is an ancient art, revived with a vengeance in the early 19th century. Recognizable by the raised seam where the edge of the mold was positioned, it often has a naive vigor and charm that make up for lack of pedigree.

Art Deco style pressed glass

Blown glass

Alarmingly delicate transparent flutes, blown glass can be stretched and shaped, and may incorporate twists and bubbles of air that flicker with miniature replicas of the light source.

Cut glass (below and right)
This is the classic medium for elaborate candelabra and ornate candlesticks, festooned with faceted droplets that sparkle and cast rainbows with the slightest movement.

Delicate blown flute

Prismatic cut facets

Typical Victorian molded glass

Antique
Ransack junk shops for affordable Victorian candlesticks in a combination of cut and pressed glass.

Cut glass column

Wooden candlesticks

Turned, painted, hand carved, or embellished with bands of brass or copper, wooden candlesticks tend to have a definite solidity and somewhat masculine character. They are indirectly descended from the medieval expedient of supporting a candle with a spike in a block of wood, or several spikes (prickets) in a circular dished tray, attached to a wooden post or block—simple devices that persisted in country areas until the

19th century. More ornate wooden candlesticks were developed from the walnut, ebony, and mahogany candle stands of the 17th and 18th centuries, which were often carved, painted, or gilded, and pillar-shaped with a rise and fall action to allow for the candle burning down. The most magnificent wooden candlesticks are the monumental torchères, taller than a man, that once illuminated castles and cathedrals.

Antique
Plain and turned candle-sticks are classic designs.

Pillars
Contemporary wooden candlesticks often have simple designs, relying on precision of craftsmanship and the natural qualities of wood to give sophistication and elegance.

Paint finishes
Sponged, stippled, or gilded, wooden candlesticks make a good subject for any paint effect.

Band of oxidized copper

Antique and modern dark wood in classic designs

Turned candlestick

Brass base

Ebony pillar

Dark paint with pale wood showing through

Ethnic

The most beautifully shaped and balanced candlesticks come from India—from tall and slender baluster stems with decorative knobs and touches of gilding, to huge open twist designs. They are sometimes painted in rich dark colors. Papier-mâché, too, may be painted with a confetti of tiny flowers enhanced with bands of gold.

Carved wood

From India and Africa come carved candlesticks washed with white to look like gesso or finely turned from dark hardwood in whimsical designs like chess pieces.

Brass trim typical of Eastern candlesticks

Triple twist carved from a single piece of wood

Gessolike effect

Ebony candlesticks from Africa

Carved and painted wood from India

Painted papier-mâché from Kashmir

Turned, lacquered wood

Floorstanding candelabra

Just the thing for a baronial mansion, floorstanding candelabra add a touch of Gothic splendor to an interior. The grandest have always been made for religious purposes, from the seven-branched paschal candlesticks that traditionally mark Easter celebrations in church, to the huge candelabra of Milan cathedral, known as the Trivulzio, which is more than 30 feet tall and embellished with flowers, people, and monsters. Most are made of metal: an adaptable material, it can be as smooth as machine production can make it, or as rough-hewn as hand shaping can achieve.

Glass draft excluder

Modern
Utter simplicity, right down to functional draft protection with a colored glass panel (right), characterizes modern manufactured candle holders.

Designer
Fanciful contemporary designs in a variety of metals take the traditional tree shape of floorstanding candelabra to the extreme.

Lengths of hammered copper tubing form stylized branches

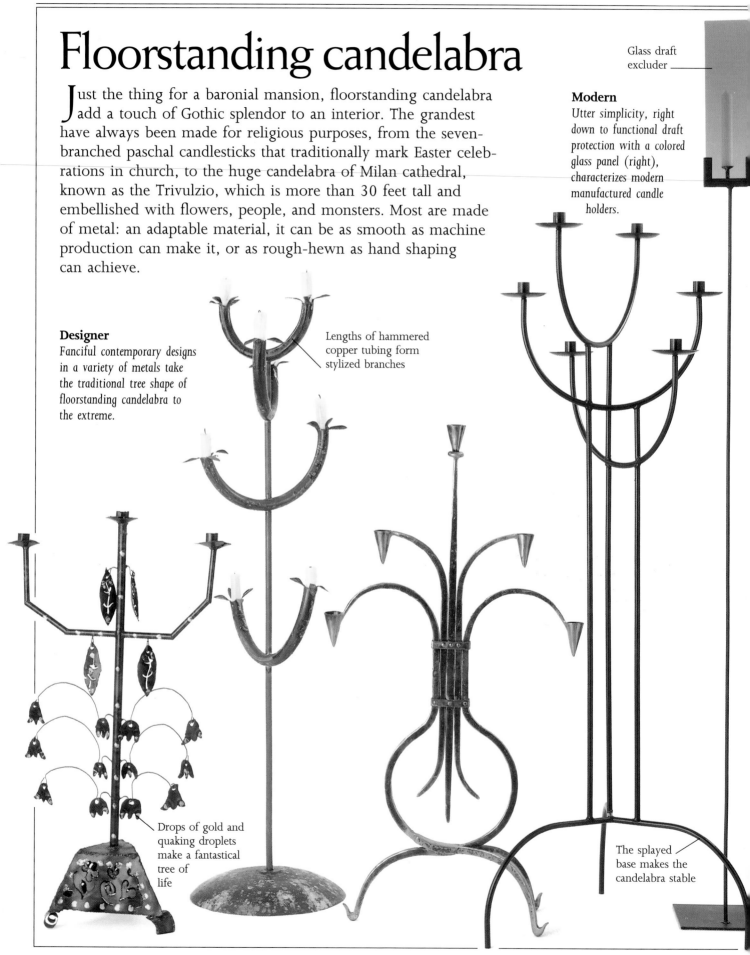

Drops of gold and quaking droplets make a fantastical tree of life

The splayed base makes the candelabra stable

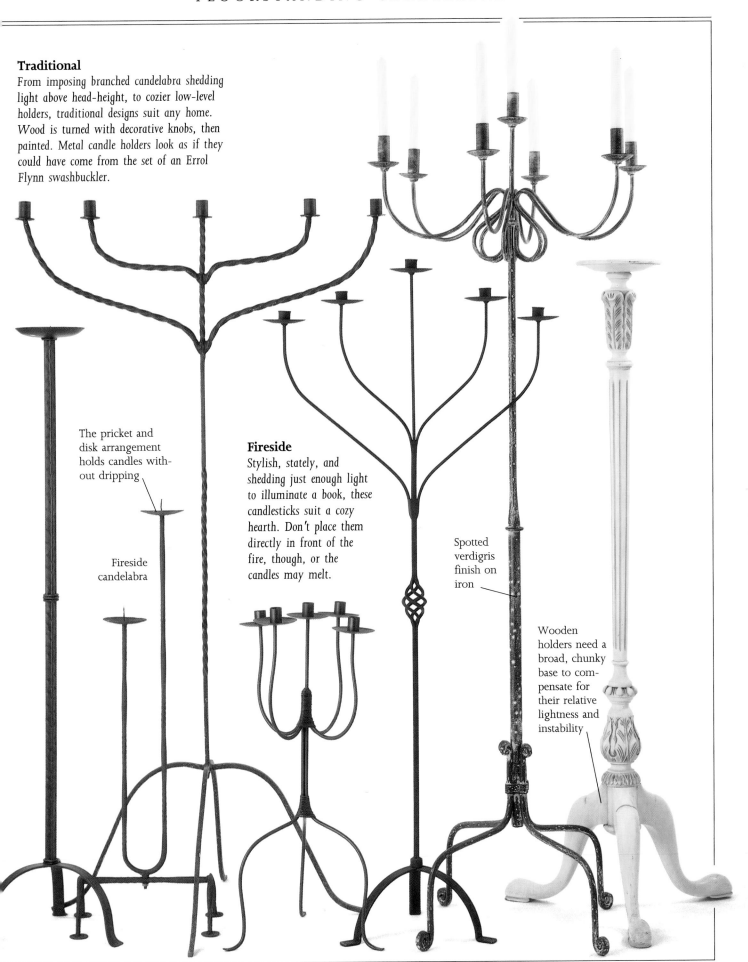

Traditional

From imposing branched candelabra shedding light above head-height, to cozier low-level holders, traditional designs suit any home. Wood is turned with decorative knobs, then painted. Metal candle holders look as if they could have come from the set of an Errol Flynn swashbuckler.

The pricket and disk arrangement holds candles without dripping

Fireside candelabra

Fireside

Stylish, stately, and shedding just enough light to illuminate a book, these candlesticks suit a cozy hearth. Don't place them directly in front of the fire, though, or the candles may melt.

Spotted verdigris finish on iron

Wooden holders need a broad, chunky base to compensate for their relative lightness and instability

Sconces

W all sconces were the great discovery of the 17th century, and in England, grand houses lined them up along their long dining halls. Initially they had reflectors of polished metal, usually silver, but gradually these were replaced with mirror glass, which reflected the flame more effectively. In the 18th century, mirror sconces were abandoned in favor of huge quantities of candles—the rich would have several dozen burning at once, held in rococo girandoles with picturesque details. Nowadays there are sconces for every mood and style, from the most earthy ethnic to pinnacles of glittering refinement.

Terra-cotta cherub

Mirrors
The standard expedient to multiply candle power, mirrors and reflector plates of polished metal have been used since the 17th century.

Verdigris duck
A naive and perky folk motif inspired by Pennsylvania Dutch domestic items.

Indian
Divali sconce

Ethnic
Divali, the Indian festival of lights, is celebrated with sconces portraying animals. The multistory pineapple is a new departure.

Traditional
Tin and iron in simple, elegant shapes.

Shaker tin sconce

Garlands
Bacchic naturalism
(right) looks at home
on a conservatory
wall, while second
empire formality
(below) is suited
to a bare neoclassic
modern interior.

Carved wood
A veritable tour de force
of the candlestick-
maker's art, this is a
fine rococo extravagance
of ribbons and musical
instruments.

Country
Verging on the folksy, hearts and
flowers are for nostalgia fanatics.

Brass panel
Entwined dolphins and
fleurs-de-lis make a
baroque plaque. Its
polished metal reflects
flickering candlelight.

Floral brass
An ornate antique sconce, probably
one of a pair, this was intended to be
attached to a wall beneath pier glasses.

Chandeliers

In the 12th century, massive hoops of iron or bronze, with multiple prickets for holding candles, hung from the ceilings of churches. Two hundred years later, brass chandeliers were surmounted by angels or saints, and often decorated with Gothic crocketing. A rope and pulley allowed them to be lowered for lighting and snuffing. The 17th century saw the creation of chandeliers with eight or more S-shaped arms curving out from a central globe. Throughout the 18th century, increasingly decorative glass chandeliers were fashionable, culminating in the brilliant colored and cut glass confections of Venice and Bohemia.

Traditional country
Simple curves topped by a nosegay of curlicues, eight cups and candle sockets to shed a respectable glow of light while avoiding the accompanying drip of wax. It is essential that chandeliers have adequate drip trays or that you use nondrip candles: dinner guests do not relish hot wax in their hair.

Drip tray

Provençal chandelier
Graceful simplicity in a swooping web of iron, a design that would adapt well to a beamed and whitewashed country setting or an urban loft with a view of rooftops.

Slender candles emphasize the sweeping curves of the chandelier

Use a strong chain, since chandeliers can be heavy

Carved wood
An energetic whirligig of fine carving, the flamboyant shape is balanced by the discreet gessolike paint finish—a design that harks back to scrolled and foliated Chippendale designs.

Stylized leaf applied to the basic structure

Ornate metal
A festive and lighthearted chandelier, this basically simple construction is enriched by a handful of applied leaves. The finish is verdigris, delicately gilded and distressed to give it an appropriate autumnal warmth.

Decorative scrolls are added once the main rod is shaped

Crown of lights
A modern interpretation of the medieval corona chandelier, this gives a gentle reminder of the original prickets. The texture of wrought iron is lost when it is painted—beeswax and turpentine prevent rust and enhance the natural character of the metal.

Accessories

Once a passion for candles has been kindled, you will find that there are all sorts of adjuncts to make them burn more prettily and ingenious ideas intended to make them behave better. Safety is also a consideration that must not be forgotten, and as a result there are gadgets that help keep candles stable and upright, and snuffers to ensure that an extinguished flame really is dead. And some things—shades or antique wick trimmers, for example—are desirable simply for the aesthetic pleasure they bring.

Drip catchers
An indispensable aid to cleaning, these protect surfaces from hot wax.

Integral snuffer

Boldly striped pleated paper shade

Shade holders
These either grip the candle with a spring or slide over the top of the candle like a hood. They hold the shade at a constant height over the flame as the candle burns down.

Gilded swags on a navy enameled shade

Candle shades (left)
Much used early in this century, shades give a dim but elegant illumination.

Antique brass snuffer

Reproduction snuffer of wrought iron

An elegant silver and
ebony snuffer

Snuffers
These douse the flame effectively and eliminate
some of the smell of extinguished candles.

Box to collect the
spent wick

Wick trimmer
Modern braided wicks need less attention
than the twisted wicks of the past, so
a trimmer is no longer a necessity.

Christmas tree holders
These grip the branches
like clothespins.

Candle boxes
Storage boxes hung on the wall
meant that candles could
always be found, and it
was obvious when
supplies were
running low.

Candle stickers
Disks of wax made for this
purpose hold the candle firmly
in place.

Foam rubber snuggers
Thin disks of foam rubber grip
the candle in its holder. Once
pressed into position, they are
not visible.

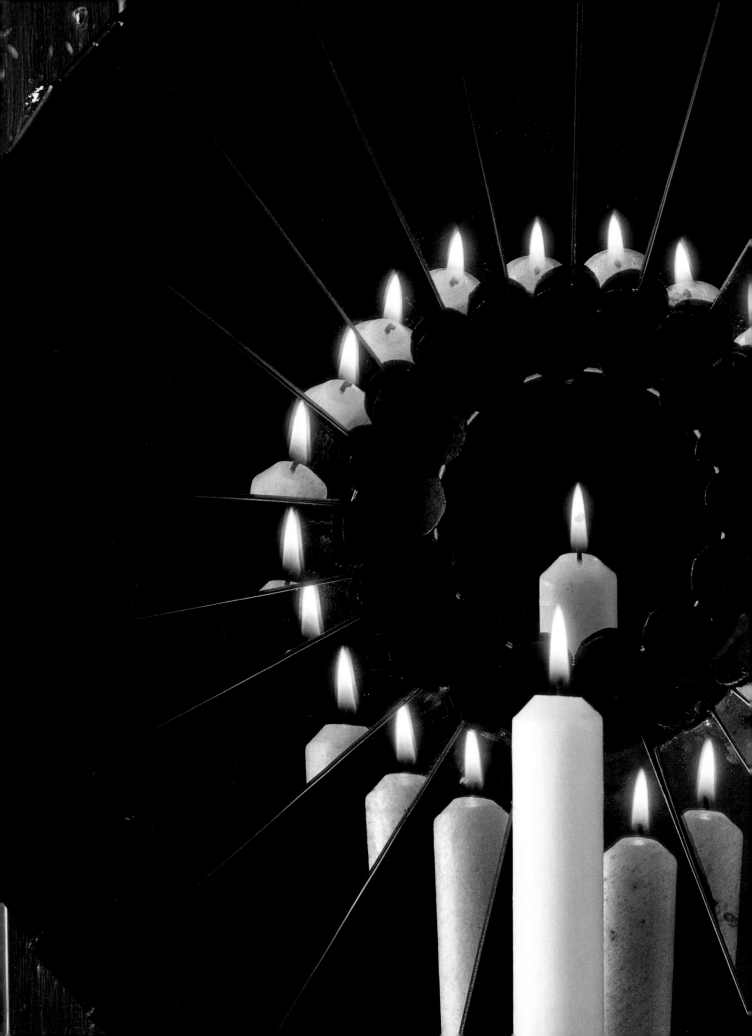

DECORATING
WITH
CANDLES

Light is the most important
decorative element in any room,
and candlelight has an unrivaled
evocative power—warming
colors create a charmed circle of
interest and benignly censor the
ugly banalities of life. Whatever
the setting, here are ideas and
inspiration for candlelit interiors
to suit any mood.

Christmas in the city

Dark, rich, baroque colors characterize Christmas in the city. The classic combination of red, green, and gold makes a festive theme upon which to play variations. An air of sophistication and opulence is needed; take the three kings rather than the manger as your cue. Fortunately, the jewels do not need to be real, and frankincense and myrrh can impart fragrance to candles rather than gracing priceless coffers. An enjoyment of the theatrical is part of this look, and an element of kitsch is not out of place. A city Christmas looks to Renaissance Italy for inspiration, drawing on the glowing brocades, intricate jewels, and dark shadows of paintings by Bellini and Titian. Go for rich, strong colors combined with glossy evergreens and a glitter of golden ornaments. For a look of sumptuous luxury, light rooms entirely by candles, with hosts of matching or theme-related candlesticks.

Baroque tabletop (left) *Gilded putti and a cornucopia of wine-dark fruit—this is a Bacchanalian interpretation of Christmas with strong Roman antecedents.*

Glittering mantelpiece (right) *A dazzle of golden candlesticks, rich reflections in a gilded mirror, and a fat swag of beribboned evergreens—these are the ingredients of a city celebration, making a defiant blaze of brightness at the very darkest time of the year.*

Christmas in the country

Simple, casual, natural—these are the words that characterize a country Christmas. The soft, subtle colors beloved by the Scandinavians—verdigris, russet, and ivory—work well with rough plaster and scrubbed wood, while the tasteful sobriety that came easily to the Shakers has a natural affinity with bone white and beeswax candles. This is an innocent Christmas, the peaceful antidote to parties, hangovers, glitter, and baubles. The ingredients are probably in front of you. Take your supplies from the woods and from your own backyard, and embellish them very simply with terra-cotta flowerpots and twine from your garden, spices and pomanders from your kitchen, and ribbons from your sewing box. Stick to uncluttered arrangements in muted colors, using natural textures to lend interest and allowing the subtle light of candles to add a warm glow.

Advent wreath (above)
A ring of oasis, crammed with the remnants of autumn richness—berries, mosses, bark, and pinecones—makes an attractive roosting place for four Advent candles, one to be burned on each of the four Sundays before Christmas.

Cottage simplicity (right)
Verdigris metal adds distinction to bowls and baskets of reindeer moss holding chunky ivory candles. This pretty Scandinavian custom is perfect for tables and windowsills.

Country cottage style

The natural materials and simple finishes of cottage style lend themselves to the gentle glow of candlelight: plain cream dipped candles and fragrant ocher beeswax are ideal partners to wood and rough plaster. There is a warmth and liveliness in candlelight that perfectly suits irregular or textured walls and weathered, functional furniture. The small focus of a candle flame is kind to country clutter, fading old garden boots and dog baskets into benign obscurity, while glancing brightly on china-filled dressers and sparkling glass. The fragile flame defies whatever weather rages outside, drawing attention inwards to safe coziness. The friendly customs of northern Europe—windows lined with lights to signify welcome to the passing stranger, or seasonal celebration to the world at large—can be rekindled in darkest Dakota.

The Shaker tradition
(left and below)
The Shakers achieved the perfect marriage of form and function, producing everyday objects of natural grace and simplicity. Typical is painted wood in a muted color paired with a sculptural minimalism of metal.

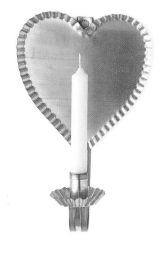

A country dresser (right)
A more eclectic interpretation of country living is given by masses of beeswax candles and rustic candlesticks of turned and painted wood, verdigris metal, and an insouciant fox prancing among earthy painted pottery.

Romantic style

Candles are synonymous with romance: their soft, glowing light suffuses the most practical interior with warmth and mystery. There is something about the little halo of candlelight that draws people together in conspiratorial closeness and focuses attention on the niceties—the glittering ensemble of glass, silver, and porcelain. Scented candles add to a general feeling of luxury; choose rich, heady fragrances such as rose, jasmine, or orchid, or the earthy wood scents of cedar or sandalwood. This is the opportunity to use your best china and finest tableware along with plenty of muted antique gilt. A tureen of floating candles illuminates food and faces at a flattering height. For a side table or in a bedroom, introduce a touch of nostalgia with artless Victoriana and drifts of white lace.

Dinner table (left)
*Dancing flames reflected in a wall of stars—
cherubs support a dish of floating candles,
and a fringe of glass beads diffuses the light.*

Lacy bedroom (above)
*An utterly romantic table: posies, bows and
family mementos. White candles add dignity
to what could be an excess of sweetness.*

Classic perfection

The ultimate in refinement, classic style is a considered look: nothing happens by accident, and good things tend to be symmetrical and come in pairs. Elegant fluted columns of silver, gilt, porphyry, marble—the materials to look for are solid, valuable, and improved by the patina of time. Ideally, the candlesticks are left to you by a wealthy ancestor with impeccable taste, but failing such good management, it is possible to find affordable antiques, occasional fakes, or even to emulate marble and lapis lazuli yourself on a plain wooden candlestick. The rich, dark colors of a gentlemen's club suit the style, as do the surprising bright colors favored by Robert Adam. Pillars, plinths, gryphons, obelisks, antique candelabra with sinuous S-shaped arms and second empire laurel wreaths are all motifs to look for, and they are appropriate partners to ornate gilt picture frames, an old master or two, or a crisp Palladian print.

Studied formality (left)

Symmetry is all: a somewhat heterogeneous ensemble of metal candlesticks, none of which is entirely classical, takes on a convincing air of the antique when arranged with exacting and formal symmetry. Dark wallpaper and a polished 18th-century table help.

Architectural echoes (above)

Grouped in front of a wall of *Adam*-ish blue, this collection of pillars and obelisks, plus a silver candelabra, has a clean sobriety. This sort of classical reference works well with the architectural print and is shown off by the sculptural swags of a muslin tablecloth.

Ethnic styles

Indigo and spice colors, handmade objects proclaiming their peculiarities, extrovert shapes and finishes—ethnic is a vigorous antidote to the clinical perfections of our machine-made world of high technology. The very presence of a finely made African basket, or a carved and painted Indian elephant, seems mutely to encourage slowing down and reverting to the simpler pleasures. The rich exuberance of Africa and India; the brilliant colors and joyous flourishes; painted tin and rainbow textiles that characterize South American style; the sobriety of Chinese lacquer and delicate basketwork; the carelessly hand-painted roses glowing from a dark background beloved by the Russians—these are all expressions of ethnic international folk art. Go for the spirit of the look, rather than slavish authenticity; you are trying to create a mood, not a museum. Be bold with your candles—massive cream church candles always look good, but experiment with bright colors and adventurous shapes.

Indian look (above)
Rich colors and patterns—paisley motifs, tiny flowers, exuberant saffron yellow, and cinnabar red—complement the solidity of carved wooden candlesticks and the vigorous simplicity of the Divali screen, the multilevel sconce essential to the festival of lights.

African look (right)
A block-printed pale indigo hanging makes a perfect backdrop to carved ebony candlesticks and a well-made Ali Baba basket. The massive black spiral candlestick gives scale and contrast to a collection of intricately carved wood and naive wrought metal.

A contemporary look

From the kitschy charms of tinsel or the casual brightness of a touch of peasant ethnicity, to the expensive handmade designer original, this is a look where anything goes. Clean electric colors make dramatic partnerships: use strongly dyed bright primary candles in simple shapes against a bold background. Or go for a more spartan style: geometric candles—spheres, pyramids, cubes, and cones—are the ideal match for a minimalist interior, and there is a wide range of shapes in black, white, cream, or gray that will complement severe monochrome interiors. Contemporary style is about having fun and trying daring contrasts. The vital accessory that can give life to an interior, a candle is not, after all, a major investment, so you can experiment with the whole spectrum of colors and every kind of shape and size.

Modern medieval (left)
Lighthearted striped arabesques cavort on this handmade wool rug and make a lively background for simple wrought iron candlesticks holding unashamedly clashing candles.

International glitter (above)
The irreverent wit of contemporary design from London and Mexico. The mirror sconce is covered in a magpie's hoard of bright bits and pieces and is comfortably at home with ethnic tin candlesticks.

THE ART OF MAKING CANDLES

Simple ingredients for a satisfying sense of achievement— even the raw materials have an earthy charm. Candle-making is fun: the rules are made to be broken, failures are not tragic, and experimentation is part of the pleasure. You can always set fire to your flawed masterpiece, and it will glow just as brightly. Here are clear, step-by-step instructions for making and decorating your own candles.

Preparing to make candles

Making your own candles is straight-forward, does not require complicated equipment, and gives a wonderful sense of achievement for very little cost or effort. It also gives you a chance to produce exactly the effects you want, to make unusual shapes, and to create a range of subtle colors that look marvelous together and can be are custom-made for your decoration and candlesticks.

BASIC EQUIPMENT
Stove or **hot plate**
Scales
Double boiler or any tall heatproof container in a pan of hot water
Newspaper and **apron**
Specific methods of candle-making may require additional equipment (see equipment listed under each method).

USEFUL INFORMATION
• 1 tbsp wax weighs about 1 oz (25g)
• 1³/₄ pts (1 liter) volume = 2 lb (900g) solid wax
• 6¹/₂ lb (3kg) wax makes 6 candles ¹/₂-³/₄ in (12-19mm) diameter and 9 in (22.5cm) long
• A container 12 in deep by 8 in wide (30 x 20cm) will take 15 lb (7kg) wax

Wax thermometer
This covers a lower temperature range than an ordinary cooking thermometer.

TYPES OF WAX

Paraffin wax
The basic wax used in candle-making, this is inexpensive and easy to work. It comes as tiny beads or pellets.

Beeswax
This is more expensive and harder to work with than paraffin wax, but a small amount can be mixed with paraffin wax to improve the quality of the candle.

Wax sheets
These are available in both beeswax and paraffin wax. Beeswax sheets often come with a honeycomb texture.

Stearin
A little is added to wax to prevent candles from dripping exces-sively. It also makes the wax opaque, helps to distribute dyes, and makes candles easier to remove from molds.

WICKS

It is important to use the correct size of wick for the thickness of candle you are making: too thick and the candle will smoke, too thin and the candle will burn with too small a flame and may go out. The sizes correspond to the diameter of a candle made of paraffin wax with up to 10 percent beeswax content: pure beeswax candles need a thicker wick.

Braided cotton wicks

Wicks for candles from $^1/_2$ in (12.5mm) to 3 in (76mm) thick.

DYES

When dyeing wax, bear in mind that the color changes as it cools. Check the final color by putting about a teaspoonful of the dyed wax in a shallow container and letting it cool for about five minutes. Then, if necessary, strengthen the color by adding dye or dilute by adding wax.

Specially made dyes
Available as powder or in blocks, these distribute quickly and easily through the wax.

Crayons
Grate or crumble these into wax.

Oil paints
Blend these to achieve subtle colors.

Fabric dye sticks
These will dissolve if grated or crumbled into wax.

GENERAL TIPS

Melting wax
Always melt wax in a container over a pan of hot water. To blend waxes and dye, melt the stearin, then add the dye and stir it in. When both have melted, add the wax, stirring as it melts. Use a thermometer to check the temperature of the wax.

Using beeswax
Beeswax is viscous and tends to stick to the mold, so use up to 10 percent beeswax or add a silicon releasing agent to help remove the candle from its mold. For any beeswax candle, whether molded, dipped, or rolled, use a thicker wick than usual.

Priming the wick
For good results, prime the wicks before making candles. Melt a little wax and immerse the wicks for about five minutes, then take them out and pull them straight. Lay them on greaseproof paper to harden.

General precautions
• Keep unused wax clean, so that candles you make later don't have dust and fluff in them.
• Never dispose of melted wax down the drain.
• Never allow wax to set in a container with a base wider than the top, since when you remelt, the wax can spurt out violently.
• If wax begins to smoke, turn off the heat, but do not touch the wax. If it catches fire, smother the flames with a lid.

Making dipped candles

A gratifyingly simple procedure, dipping requires only basic ingredients and a modicum of patience. You will need a container deeper than the height of the finished candle, which necessitates a huge volume of wax—a container 12 in (30cm) deep by 8 in (20cm) wide will hold about 15 lb (7kg) of wax. Beeswax is expensive to use in such quantities, but paraffin wax is more affordable. Dipped candles are usually made in pairs, but beware: the candles in a pair have a fatal attraction to each other—if they can weld together, they will, so you may find it easier to make candles singly at first. Dipping is a time-consuming process, so it is a good idea to make a batch of three or four individual candles or pairs at a time.

You will need

About 3 lb (1.4kg) stearin (optional)
½ tsp dye (optional)
About 15 lb (7kg) paraffin wax, more if your container is over 8 in (20cm) in diameter
¾ lb (350g) beeswax (optional)
Four 24 in (60cm) lengths of ½ in wick
Double boiler or dipping can, at least 12 in (30cm) tall
Wax thermometer
Spoon or stick for stirring
Tall container of cold water
Hooks or a rod for hanging candles to dry
Newspaper or bowl to catch drips

1 Heat the stearin, stirring it as it melts, then add the dye, if you are using it. Add the wax to a depth of about 10 in (25cm) and heat to 160°F (71°C), stirring as it melts. Prime the wicks (see page 65).

2 Hold the wick in the middle and dip the two ends into the wax to a depth of about 10 in (25cm) with a swift, smooth movement, leaving a clear area of about 4 in (10cm) in the middle.

3 Dip the wick in cold water to cool it, then hang it up to dry, making sure that the ends do not touch. Dip the remaining wicks in wax, then water.

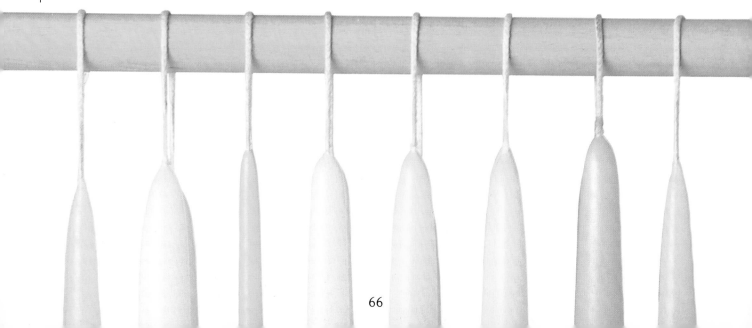

4 Continue dipping the candles in the wax followed by water, allowing them to dry for about a minute between each dip until they are the desired thickness. They will probably need at least 20 dips.

5 Heat the wax to 180°F (82°C) and dip each pair of candles twice for three seconds, allowing them to cool for a minute in between to give a smooth finish. Leave for at least an hour before burning.

OVERDIPPING IN COLOR

White candles can be overdipped in an outer coating of tinted wax. Coated candles have a more intense color than solid-color candles and do not fade as quickly. To overdip, melt a little dye and wax together and heat a deep pan of water almost to boiling. Pour the wax slowly onto the hot water to prevent bubbles from forming in the floating wax (they have an unattractive similarity to acne on a candle). Hold the candles by the wick and dip them up to the wick. Let them cool, then repeat until you obtain the color you desire.

STRIPED CANDLES

For a striped candle with four bands of color, heat four pans of water and float wax and dye in different colors, ranging from light to dark, in each pan. Dip the candle twice in the lightest color up to the wick, allowing it to dry after each dip. Next, dip it twice in the second-palest color to about three quarters of its length, letting it dry between dips. Then dip it twice in the third color to half its length, and finally dip it in the darkest color to a quarter of its length.

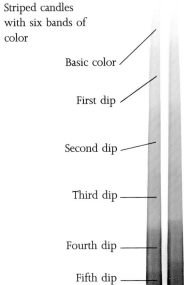

Striped candles with six bands of color

Basic color

First dip

Second dip

Third dip

Fourth dip

Fifth dip

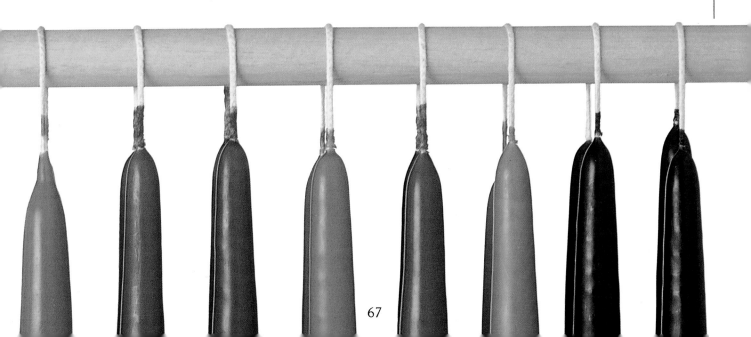

Making molded candles

Made by pouring molten wax into a prepared container, molded candles are easy to make. Candle-makers' supply stores sell molds in glass, plastic, rubber, or metal, some in shapes such as spheres, that come apart in the middle to release the candle. Once you start thinking along candle-making lines, you will find all sorts of possibilities—metal muffin tins and petits fours molds, for example, offer interesting shapes and sizes. Candle wax has an amazing ability to pick up the minutest imperfection on the surface of a mold, so unless the mold is perfectly smooth, brush cooking oil over the inside.

You will need

1 oz (25g) stearin (not for a rubber mold)
¹/₂ tsp dye (optional)
7 oz (225g) paraffin wax
1 in wick, 16 in (40cm) long
Wax thermometer
Double boiler (or saucepan and container)
Spoon or stick for stirring
Mold
Cooking oil and brush (optional)
Mold seal (or chewing gum)
Pencil or small knitting needle
Cardboard
Scissors
Deep container of cold water

1 Heat the stearin. When it has melted, add the dye and stir until the mixture is thoroughly blended.

2 Add 11 tablespoons of paraffin wax and allow the mixture to melt, stirring occasionally. Prime the wicks (see page 65). Put the thermometer into the wax.

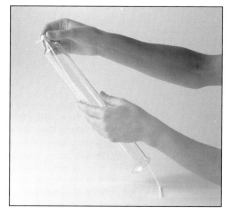

3 Lightly oil the mold, if necessary, then thread the wick through the hole at the base and cover it with enough mold seal to make a watertight seal.

4 Pull the wick taut and tie the loose end to a pencil or knitting needle to hold it in place down the center of the mold. Cut a cardboard collar to hold the mold upright in the container of cold water.

5 When the wax reaches 180°F (82°C), pour it carefully into the mold, trickling it down the side to prevent it from frothing up. After a minute or two, tap the mold to release any air bubbles.

6 Place the mold in a deep container of cold water to cool the wax, making sure that no water splashes into the wax. Hold the mold vertical by using the cardboard collar.

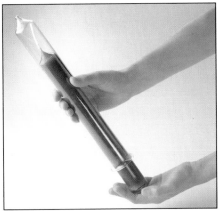

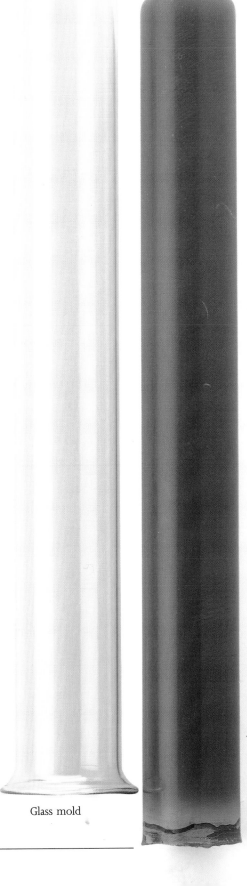

7 *The wax shrinks as it cools, and after about an hour there will be a well around the wick at the top. Pierce the surface film, and top off the well with molten wax, being careful not to let it flood over onto the surrounding solidified wax.*

8 *When the candle has set, take the mold out of the water and remove the seal. Hold the mold upside down and let the candle slide out. Trim the wick, then level the base of the candle by holding it briefly against the base of a heated saucepan.*

USING OTHER TYPES OF MOLDS

Look around kitchen supply stores for containers to use as molds: you can use anything provided it will withstand hot wax and that it is wider at the top than at the base, so that the candle can slide out when it has set. If you can make a small hole in the base to accommodate the wick, so much the better. If not, use a wicking needle longer than the height of your candle to thread the wick through the center of the candle when it is set.

To use a rubber mold, melt the wax and dye together, but don't use stearin, since it rots the rubber. As the candle sets, break the surface skin of the wax frequently and top off with molten wax after about two hours. To remove it from the mold, smear dishwashing liquid over the outside and peel the mold back carefully.

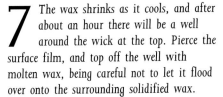

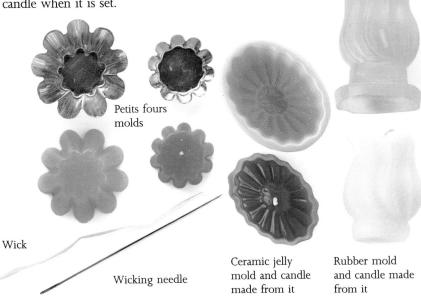

Petits fours molds

Wick

Wicking needle

Ceramic jelly mold and candle made from it

Rubber mold and candle made from it

Glass mold

Making rolled candles

Rolled candles are the easiest of all to make and may not even require a heat source, which means that children can make their own candles. A thin sheet of wax is simply rolled up around a wick. Sheets of beeswax are the easiest to work with—they are generally tan-colored, with a honeycomb texture. Paraffin wax is less malleable than beeswax, so you may need to warm the sheet first to avoid cracking it when you roll it. To warm it, leave it on top of a radiator or in a very low oven for a few minutes, or carefully play a hair dryer over it until the wax softens.

You will need
Scissors or blade and ruler
1 sheet of beeswax or
1 sheet of paraffin wax $^1/_8$ in (2-3mm) thick
$^1/_2$ in (12.5mm) wick, 8 in (20cm) long

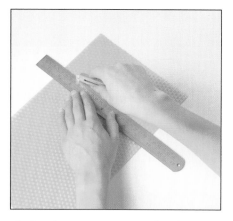

1 Cut the wax into a rectangle. The length of the short sides will be the height of your candle, while that of the long sides determines its thickness.

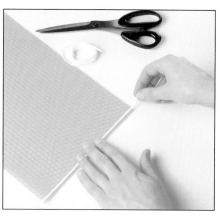

2 Cut the wick 1 in (2cm) longer than the narrow side of the wax rectangle and gently press it into the wax along one of the short sides.

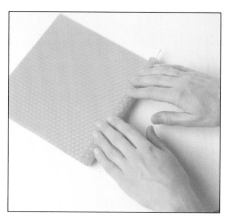

3 Roll up the wax tightly to enclose the wick in the middle. Ensure that the wick is closely and evenly held with the first turn. The more tightly you roll, the longer the candle will burn.

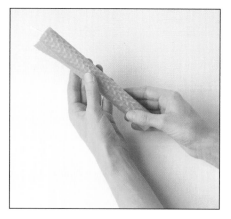

4 When the candle is the thickness you want, cut off any surplus wax parallel to the wick using scissors or a blade and ruler. Press the cut edge into the roll to give a neat finish.

SPIRAL CANDLES
Make a spiral candle by cutting the sheet of wax into a triangle. Trim a tiny amount from the corner that will form the top of the candle, then place the wick along the edge and roll the wax as before. A tall narrow triangle will give a tall spiral candle, while a broad triangle will produce a conical one.

Rolled candle

Spiral candles

Making scented candles

One of the pleasures of making your own candles is that of imparting a delicious fragrance to the room when they burn. Any store that sells candle supplies will have a range of special scented oils with which you can concoct the perfect scent. According to aromatherapists, smells can soothe or revitalize—certainly sensuous wafts of sandalwood or refreshing whiffs of lavender promote a feeling of well-being. In addition, the scent of citronella has useful mosquito and gnat deterrent qualities, which could prevent you from being insect food when enjoying a candlelit dinner outside. There are four ways of scenting candles, all very simple—it is worth the little additional effort to add this extra dimension to your candles.

You will need
Candle scents or essential oils or herbs or aromatic flowers

Oil of juniper

Lavender flowers

Lemon verbena leaves

Candle scents

QUICK METHOD
The easiest way of adding scent to a candle is simply to put a few drops of scented oil around the burning wick—an effect that will not last long, but will give a powerful burst of fragrance.

SCENTING THE WICK
For a reasonably long-lasting fragrance, melt a little wax and add a few drops of scent. Prime a handful of wicks (*see page 65*) in this for about 20 minutes, then make candles using any of the techniques described on pages 66 to 70.

SCENTING THE WAX
For the most enduring scent, impregnate the wax as you make the candles. Melt the wax and stearin (*see page 65*), then add a few drops of scent—four or five drops to a pound is enough; more may mottle the candles. Blend the mixture well, then dip or mold the candles as usual.

USING HERBS AND FLOWERS
Dried and fresh herbs and flowers incorporated into molten wax release a slight fragrance as they burn, which can be heightened by adding a few drops of matching scent. Melt wax and stearin, then add a bunch of herbs and leave for 45 minutes, keeping the temperature at about 180°F (75°C). Remove the herbs, add a little scent if desired, and make candles by dipping or molding.

Jasmine-scented candle

Rose-scented candle

Dropper for scents and oils

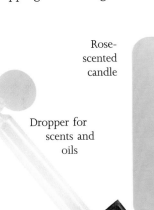

Pressed flower candles

With a steady hand and a little patience, the flowers of summer can be pressed and then set on candles to bloom again long after the first frosts. Collect your plant material when it is fresh and open, before there is any hint of drooping petals, and make sure that it is dry and free of insects. Use a flower press, or place each item face down on two layers of tissue or blotting paper laid smoothly between the pages of a hefty book. Restrict yourself to one type of plant per sheet, and make sure that the flowers or leaves do not overlap, or they will stick to each other. Flatten the flowers slightly with your fingers and top with another two pieces of tissue. Shut the book gently, put another on top, and leave for at least a week. It takes very little practice to become proficient at decorating candles with pressed flowers. Large round and square pillar candles are the easiest to handle, and a simple pressed garland around the base will be enough for you to master the technique.

You will need

Teaspoon
Iron or hot plate
Selection of pressed flowers and leaves
Tissue paper
White pillar candle
Cloth or nonroll surface
Tweezers
For overdipping: Double boiler (or saucepan and container), 2 lb (1kg) paraffin wax, spoon or stick for stirring, 2-3 drops of candle scent (optional), pliers

1 Heat the paraffin wax gently over a saucepan of hot water, stirring occasionally until it has melted.

2 Add the candle scent if you want to scent the candles as you dip them. Meanwhile, heat the bowl of a teaspoon on an iron or hot plate.

3 Arrange the pressed flowers on a sheet of tissue paper to give an idea of the finished design. Lay the candle on a cloth and carefully position one of the larger elements against the side of the candle.

4 Delicately press all parts of the flower onto the candle with the heated spoon, rolling the bowl gently over the surface of the flower.

5 Carefully build up the design one item at a time, positioning each flower or leaf accurately, then ironing gently over it with the heated spoon to fix it in place with melted wax.

6 Once the arrangement is complete, seal the candle by overdipping it. Hold it firmly by the wick (you may need pliers if the wick is short) and immerse it in the hot wax.

7 Lift the candle out after about three seconds and allow it to dry. Leave it for at least an hour before burning.

Floral diversity
Delicately colored and graphic in shape, pressed flowers embellish candles with pleasing effects, from a geometric trellis pattern to naturalistic garlands.

Painting techniques

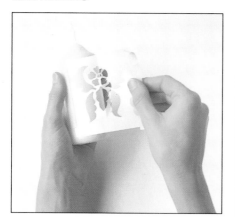

For a special occasion or to suit a very splendid candlestick, it is surprisingly easy to decorate candles. Bold designs can be applied with stencils—numbers for a birthday candle, snowflakes and stars on a Christmas candle, hearts and even initials for Valentine's Day. Roman numerals and horizontal stripes, guided with masking tape, make an effective but not too accurate medieval timepiece. Sponging with layers of color is quick and easy and makes for subtle cloudy shades and textures. A veil of gold sponged on the top looks rich and festive. It is simplest to work on a sturdy white candle using poster paint or gouache.

You will need
Stenciling: Stencil, masking tape, paints, dishwashing liquid, small cosmetic sponge, equipment and paraffin wax for overdipping
Sponging: Paints, dishwashing liquid, small cosmetic sponge, equipment and paraffin wax for overdipping
Freehand painting: Paints, dishwashing liquid, medium-sized artist's brush, equipment and paraffin wax for overdipping

STENCILING

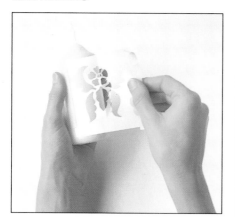

1 Stick one edge of a stencil to the candle with masking tape. Pull the stencil around the candle to ensure a snug fit, then tape down the other side.

2 Mix the paint with water and a drop or two of dishwashing liquid, to the consistency of thick cream. Dab on a fine layer of color with a cosmetic sponge.

3 If the base color lacks subtlety or depth, or if you want to highlight particular areas or outlines, dab on a toning or contrasting color.

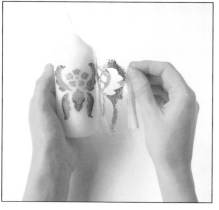

4 When the paint is completely dry, peel off the masking tape and carefully remove the stencil. Avoid touching the painted area, and seal the design by overdipping (see page 73, steps 6-7).

Strong, bold shapes are typical of stenciled patterns

Stenciled pattern

SPONGING

1 Mix paint with a little water and dishwashing liquid, and dab color lightly over the sides and top of the candle with a sponge. *Avoid getting paint on the wick.*

2 *When the first color is dry, repeat the process with a toning color. Add a third color for extra richness. Overdip in paraffin wax (see page 73, steps 6-7).*

Use gold paint for the third coat on a sponged candle to achieve something positively baroque

FREEHAND PAINTING

Mix paint with water and dishwashing liquid to the consistency of thin cream, and with a medium-sized artist's brush, paint all over the candle. Overdip in paraffin wax (see page 73, steps 6-7).

Take inspiration from ceramics, fabrics or wall-paper patterns. Bold irregular peasant designs are easier than crisp Chippendale

Freehand painting

Gold stippling

Freehand dots and stripes

Rhythmic, fluent painting looks good

Freehand design

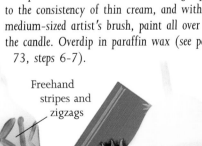

Freehand stripes and zigzags

Mixed media

Generally, the simpler a candle the better, but there are times when a fit of creativity demands something a little more decorative, and a candle is a compliant sculptural medium for experimentation. It is a good idea to remember that you are not creating a permanent work of art, so your inspiration need be only a passing whim or fanciful idea. Watch flammable materials vigilantly, and avoid anything likely to give off toxic fumes. With thicker candles, only the wick area burns, and your designs may glow with the flame like stained glass.

You will need

Fresh foliage: Leaves, pins, raffia, flowers
Carving: Equipment, wax, and dye for overdipping; lino cutting tool, paint, dishwashing liquid, fine paintbrush
Foil: Colored foil or metallic paper, scissors, teaspoon, iron or hot plate, sequins, pins or glue
Tissue: Tissue paper, printer's block and ink pad, teaspoon, iron or hot plate; equipment and wax for overdipping

FRESH FOLIAGE

1 Select a few unblemished ivy leaves and pin them in position around the base of a thick candle. "Skeleton" leaves also look very pretty.

2 Wrap some raffia around the candle to hold the leaves in place, tie it in a bow, then remove the pins. Tuck a tiny posy of flowers into the raffia.

A festive and ephemeral confection of ivy, raffia, and *Chaenomeles*.

CARVING

1 Dip a candle in wax of a strong, contrasting color floating on hot water (*see page 67*) to get a deep, smooth overlay. Allow the wax to cool completely.

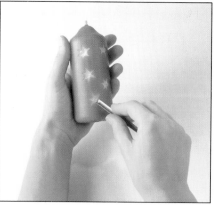

2 Using a lino cutting tool, carefully chisel out stars all over the candle, carving through the outer coating of wax to reveal the color beneath.

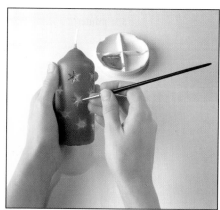

3 For a festive touch, mix a little gold paint with water and a drop of dishwashing liquid, and paint each star gold using a fine paintbrush.

APPLYING FOIL

A magpie's collection of metallic paper and sequins is perfect for Halloween or a pop Christmas

1 Cut shapes of colored foil or metallic paper—bold geometric shapes are easiest to begin with.

2 Heat a teaspoon against an iron or hot plate, position each piece of foil and press it in place with the hot spoon. Finally, glue or pin on a few sequins.

Carved stripes

APPLYING TISSUE PAPER

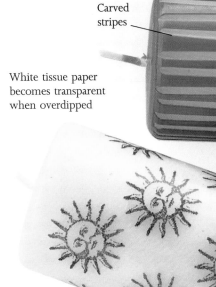

White tissue paper becomes transparent when overdipped

1 Cut tissue paper to fit around your candle. Use patterned paper or decorate your own—here a pattern is stamped with a printer's block.

2 Heat a teaspoon against an iron or hot plate, then wrap the tissue around the candle and iron over it with the spoon. Seal by overdipping (see page 73, steps 6-7).

Strips of colored tissue paper

Carved shapes can be painted or left so that the base color shows through

Carved and painted stars

Patterned paper

Carved decorations

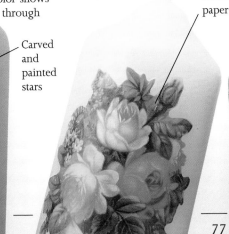

List of suppliers

Candles and candlesticks

American Candle Classics
19 East Martin St.
Allentown
Pa. 18103
(215) 791-0698
Candles, votives. Mail order

Colonial Williamsburg Foundation
201 5th Avenue
Williamsburg
Va. 23185
(804) 220-7645
Candlesticks. Mail order

Conran's Habitat
10 Astor Place
New York
N.Y. 10003
(800) 346-1925
Candles, candlesticks, sconces, shades

Cumberland General Store
Route 3, Box 81
Crossville
Tenn. 38555
(615) 484-8481
Beeswax, sconces. Mail order

The Edison Institute
20900 Oakwood Boulevard
Dearborn
Mich. 48121-1970
(313) 271-1620
Candlesticks. Mail order

The Horchow Collection
Box 620048
Dallas
Texas 75262-0048
(800) 527-0303
Sconces, votive candles, holders, candlesticks. Mail order

Hurley Patentee Manor
464 Old Route 209
Hurley
N.Y. 12443
(914) 331-5414
Candlesticks, sconces. Mail order

Independence Forge
Route 1, Box 1-C
Whitakers
N.C. 27891
(919) 437-2931
Hand-crafted chandeliers. Mail order

Jori Pewter Cupboard
1776 Easton Road
Doylestown
Pa. 18901
(215) 345-8891
Pewter candlesticks and sconces. Mail order

Lillian Vernon Corp.
Virginia Beach
Va. 23479-0002
(914) 633-6300
Candles, sconces, votive candle holders, lanterns. Mail order

The Metropolitan Museum of Art
Museum Gift Shop
5th Avenue at 82 St.
New York
N.Y. 10028
(212) 570-3726
Reproduction candlesticks and sconces. Mail order

Museum of Modern Art Shop
11 West 53 St.
New York
N.Y. 10019
(212) 767-1050
Candle holders, candlesticks. Mail order

Pier One Imports
Box 961020
Fort Worth
Texas 76161-0020
(800) 447-4371 for store nearest you
Candles, outdoor torches, citronella candles, tapers, pillar candles, candlesticks, sconces

Period Lighting Fixtures
1 West Main St.
Chester
Conn. 06412
(203) 526-3690
Sconces, chandeliers. Mail order

Pottery Barn
Mail Order Department
Box 7044
San Francisco
Calif. 94120-7044
(415) 421-3400
Candles, candlesticks, candle holders. Mail order

The Shoemakers
Box 28
Oley
Pa. 10547
(215) 689-5022
Hand-dipped scented candles, beeswax candles, firestarters, accessories. Mail order

Spiegel
Box 6340
Chicago
Ill. 60680
(800) 345-4500
Candlesticks, sconces. Mail order

Sunset Woodworks
2012 Sunset Drive
Owosso
Mich. 48867
(517) 725-5762
Candle boxes. Mail order

The Tinhorn
1852 Forest Lane lane
Crown Point
Ind. 46307
(219) 988-3332
Tin chandeliers, lanterns, sconces. Mail order

Whitney Museum of American Art
943 Madison Avenue
New York
N.Y. 10021
(212) 570-3600
Candlesticks, candle holders. Mail order

Winterthur Museum Reproductions
Winterthur
Delaware 19735
(302) 888-4600
Candlesticks, sconces. Mail order

Yankee Candle Company
Route 5
South Deerfield
Mass. 01373
(800) 243-1776
Scented candles, country-style candles in jars, tapers, votives, pillars, novelty candles. Mail order

Candle-making supplies

Chaselle Arts & Crafts
9645 Gerwig Street
Columbia
Md. 21046
(301) 381-0828
Candle-making supplies. Mail order

The Crafts Studio
222 Maple Avenue West
Vienna
Va. 22180
(703) 938-8111
Wax, coloring, scents, wicking

Hobby Company of San Fransisco
5150 Geary Boulevard
San Francisco
Calif. 94118
(415) 386-2802
Wax, coloring, wicking

Hobby Hut
2835 Nostrand Avenue
Brooklyn
N.Y. 11229
(718) 338-2554
Wax, wicking, scents, starter kits

S & S Arts & Crafts
Box 513
Colchester
Conn. 06415-0513
(800) 243-9232
Wax, fragrances, honeycomb wax, wicking, candle-making kits, coloring, kits for sconces and candelabra. Mail order

Vanguard Crafts Inc.
Box 340170
Brooklyn
N.Y. 11234
(718) 377-5188
Wax, bulk packs, molds, scents, wicking, honeycomb wax. Mail order

Williamsburg Soap & Candle
7521 Richmond Road
Williamsburg
Va. 23188
(804) 564-3354
Candle-making supplies. Mail order

Index

Acknowledgments

Dorling Kindersley would like to thank Karen Ward for design help, Karl Adamson for photographic assistance, Hilary Bird for the index, and all staff members who kindly lent candlesticks for photography.

We are particularly grateful to the following people for their help in supplying props for photography: Pauline Sherman, Glynn Lowe and Stephanie Thomson at Candlewick Green, Chris Ryan and Louis Spear at The Candle Shop, Nick Gaiger at Nice Irma's and Saira Joshi at Thomas Goode.

Other suppliers who lent props include: Acres Farm, Anne's, J. Bostock & Associates, Candle Makers Supplies, Carless & Grey, Casa Pupo, The Conran Shop, Davies, Designer's Guild, Divine Lights, Fergus Cochrane, The General Trading Company, Global Village, Gore Booker, Judy Greenwood, Habitat, Mexique, Molton Brown, Neal Street East, Overmantels, Jane Packer, Peepul Tree Trading, Perfect Glass Shop, Prices

Candles, R. G. Scrutton, The Shaker Shop, The Study, Kenneth Turner, Verandah, Keith Watson, Ann Wood, Steve Wright, Zawadi.

Stylist for pages 52-61: Cherry Frost.

Picture credits
Key: t = top; b = bottom
The National Gallery, 6, 7t; Fine Art Photographs, 7b; The Mansell Collection, 8t; Prices Candles, 8b; The Tate Gallery, 9.

Author's acknowledgments
I would like to thank Clive Streeter and Karl Adamson for their patient ingenuity and ability to create sunshine with a light bulb, Daphne and Anne-Marie, who kept hope glowing in darker moments, Claire for her competence with both words and wax, and Sarah, who juggled successfully with the look of it all. Many people waxed lyrical and enlightening along the way—particularly Daphne Dormer, George Carter, Bridget Bodoano at Conran, Nana Laye at Dansk Import, Katya Dumonde, Steve Wright and Jane Packer. David Constable at Candle Makers Supplies made me watch a most illuminating video, the people at The Candle Shop, and Pauline Sherman at Candlewick Green shed what light they could. And Hester Page at Country Living burned the candle at both ends in a characteristic effort to lighten one's darkness.

TINY THINGS, BIG IMPACTS

PLANKTON

Written by John Wood

KidHaven
PUBLISHING

Published in 2020 by
**KidHaven Publishing, an Imprint of
Greenhaven Publishing, LLC**
353 3rd Avenue
Suite 255
New York, NY 10010

© 2020 Booklife Publishing

This edition is published by arrangement with Booklife Publishing

Edited by: Holly Duhig
Designed by: Amy Li

Cataloging-in-Publication Data

Names: Wood, John.
Title: Plankton / John Wood.
Description: New York : KidHaven Publishing, 2020. | Series: Tiny things, big impacts | Includes glossary and index.
Identifiers: ISBN 9781534532854 (pbk.) | ISBN 9781534532878 (library bound) | ISBN 9781534532861 (6 pack) | ISBN 9781534532885 (ebook)
Subjects: LCSH: Plankton--Juvenile literature.
Classification: LCC QH91.A1 W663 2020 | DDC 578.76 --dc23

Printed in the United States of America

CPSIA compliance information: Batch #BW20KL: For further information contact Greenhaven Publishing LLC, New York, New York at 1-844-317-7404.

Please visit our website, www.greenhavenpublishing.com. For a free color catalog of all our high-quality books, call toll free 1-844-317-7404 or fax 1-844-317-7405.

PHOTO CREDITS

All images are courtesy of Shutterstock.com, unless stated otherwise.

Cover – shanghaiface, Rich Carey, Borders & Plankton – shanghaiface, natchapohn, 1 – Rich Carey, 4 – science photo, Rattiya Thongdumhyu, ivivolk, 5 – Choksawatdikorn, Ihor Bondarenko, 6 – Alfmaler, Maquiladora, mlorenz, 7 – stocker1970, bluehand, Neirfy, 8 – Dmytro Pylypenko, Castleski, kajornyot wildlife photography, 9 – Joe Morris 917, I.Noyan Yilmaz, Bruce Raynor, 10 – Rich Carey, ExpressVectors, Veronika M, 11 – khlongwangchao, kl_foto, 12 – STILLFX, Here, artjazz, superjoseph, Borysevych.com, 13 – bluehand, Fiona Ayerst, 14 – Wannc, richardjohnson, 15 – Filipe Frazao, Damsea, 16 –NoDenmand, Fleur_de_papier, timsimages, Elnur, 17 – science photo, Rattiya Thongdumhyu, Stubblefield Photography, 18 – Pavlo S, NirvaNas, Oliver Hoffmann, Sabina Zak, 19 – donfiore, Lebendkulturen.de, 20 – BortN66, Rattiya Thongdumhyu, Robert Adrian Hillman, science photo, michaeljung, STILLFX Here, 21 – robert_s, Svetlana Turchenick, 22 – Kenny, Here, STILLFX, eggeegg, 23 – Nadia Snopek, Nikolaeva, Sujono sujono, Kieu images, 24 – wikipedia public domain, Ioana Filipas, 25 – Alfred Rowan, Ilya Sviridenko, 26 – Ramona Heim, Michael Gancharuk, 27 – wikipedia public domain, Dmitri Ma, 28 – Picsfive, Rich Carey, 29 – saraporn, chinahbzyg, 30 – anweber, Lebendkulturen.de

PLANKTON

CONTENTS:

WORDS THAT LOOK LIKE THIS ARE EXPLAINED IN THE GLOSSARY ON PAGE 31.

MEET THE PLANKTON

These are plankton. Plankton live in water, and they come in all sorts of different shapes and sizes. A lot of plankton are so small that they can only be seen through a **microscope**. However, even though they are tiny, plankton change the world every day. They might seem unimportant, but without them our lives would be very different indeed.

Plants and Animals

There are two different types of plankton. Phytoplankton (say: fi-toe-plank-tun) are like plants. They are often called algae. Zooplankton are animals. Most are too small to be seen, although some can grow quite big.

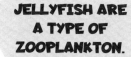

JELLYFISH ARE A TYPE OF ZOOPLANKTON.

Float On

Plankton are mostly carried around by ocean **currents**, rather than doing all the swimming themselves. Some plankton, such as jellyfish and other zooplankton, can swim up and down or push themselves forward with a burst of air. However, most of their movement comes from the currents.

A Copepod Under a Microscope

COPEPODS ARE A TYPE OF ZOOPLANKTON. THERE ARE MORE COPEPODS IN THE WORLD THAN THERE ARE INSECTS.

Algae on a Lake

Phytoplankton, or algae, mostly float on top of water, where there is more sunlight. Zooplankton can be found throughout the ocean, although most of them live near the top, eating the phytoplankton. Some animals begin life as zooplankton and change into something different later on. These are called meroplankton.

A WORLD WITHOUT
PLANKTON

The Food Chain

A food chain shows what eats what in the animal world. Food chains start with something that makes the food. This is usually a plant. Plants are eaten by animals called herbivores. Animals that eat other animals are called carnivores.

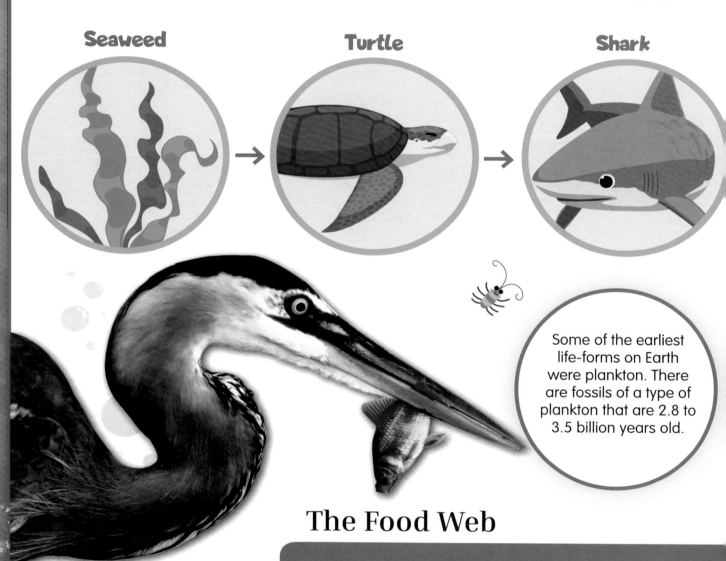

Seaweed → **Turtle** → **Shark**

Some of the earliest life-forms on Earth were plankton. There are fossils of a type of plankton that are 2.8 to 3.5 billion years old.

The Food Web

If lots of food chains are joined up, a food web is created. This looks a lot more complicated. All animals, including humans, are connected by the world's food web. Any changes to one part of the web can affect other animals, too.

Plankton in the Food Web

Phytoplankton are at the start of the food web for all animals that live in water. This means they are very important. Without plankton, herbivores wouldn't have anything to eat. If the herbivores starved, then carnivores wouldn't have anything to eat either.

EVERYTHING THAT LIVES IN THE WATER NEEDS PLANKTON – EVEN THE BIGGER ANIMALS.

Parting with Plankton

If all the plankton disappeared tomorrow, nobody knows what would happen for sure. Maybe humans would find a way to replace plankton and solve all the problems. But what if we couldn't? Throughout this book, we are going to take a look at what might happen in a world without plankton.

THE LAST BLUE WHALE

Daily News

Since 1928

LAST BLUE WHALE EATS EVERYTHING!

By J. Pointer

Since the plankton disappeared, blue whales have had nothing to eat. After disappearing one by one, the last blue whale is now being kept alive by a nearby school cafeteria. The whale, nicknamed "Fatty" by the children, eats a huge amount of fish. "We are going to run out of food!" said Emilie, the head cafeteria worker. "We need the plankton back!"

I interviewed one of the children walking by, and asked him his thoughts on the newest arrival to the school. "I love him. He is eating all the terrible school food. I'm surprised he hasn't been sick yet — all the other children have. I just don't want to be around when the vomit comes."

After this encounter, I went to find the cook. After tracking the pungent, unmistakable scent of burnt carrots, the cook was found in the kitchen. "Fatty is eating all of the school food," she said. *More on page 14.*

Whales and Plankton

Blue whales are the biggest animals ever to have lived on Earth. However, they eat very small animals – a type of zooplankton called krill.

KRILL ARE AROUND 2 INCHES (5 CM) LONG. BLUE WHALES ARE AROUND 100 FEET (30 M) LONG.

Blue whales do not have teeth. Instead the inside of their mouths are covered with **baleen plates**. This makes it easy to eat zooplankton, but difficult to eat much else. If plankton disappeared, even giant animals like blue whales wouldn't survive.

A blue whale's heart can weigh as much as a car.

Baleen Plates

Sometimes whales can eat around 7,940 pounds (3,600 kg) of zooplankton a day.

Animal Lovers

Blue whales are beautiful and intelligent animals. They are the biggest animals on the planet, and they even sing whale songs underwater. Losing plankton means losing animals such as whales. This would make the world a lot less interesting indeed.

Krill

NO FISH
ON THE MENU

Green Hills Primary School
Tel: 636-555-3226

Dear Parent or Guardian,

I am writing this letter to tell you that there will be no more fish to eat at lunchtime. This is because all the fish are gone. Here is a list of changes to the lunchtime menu:

Tuesday: Instead of fish fingers, we will now have broccoli stew with extra broccoli.
Friday: Instead of fried fish, we will now have spinach surprise.

Yours sincerely,

Ms. Pippengill
Principal

MANY FISH EAT ALGAE.

Back to the Food Web

Everything is connected to the food web, even humans. No plankton means there will be no small fish. No small fish means that there won't be any big fish for humans to eat.

Fishing Boat

Fish Around the World

Humans eat a lot of fish. There are around 4.6 million fishing boats sailing around the world and catching fish. Some of those boats are very big and catch a lot of fish. Without plankton, a lot of our food would be gone.

Fish are often cheaper than meat, so they are an important food for people who don't have a lot of money, especially in less **economically** developed countries. These countries sell a lot of fish around the world and make a lot of money. Without this money, people would be poorer.

Over 110 million tons of fish are eaten every year around the world.

VACATIONS

"HI GUYS, WELCOME TO MY CHANNEL! THIS WAS GOING TO BE A VIDEO ABOUT MY VACATION AT THE GREAT BARRIER REEF WITH MY PARENTS, BUT THEY TOLD ME THAT IT'S GONE! APPARENTLY WHEN THOSE TINY PLANKTON DISAPPEARED, SO DID A BUNCH OF OTHER STUFF!"

The biggest coral reef in the world is the Great Barrier Reef in Australia.

Coral Reefs

Without plankton, many beautiful parts of the world would also disappear. For example, coral reefs need plankton to survive.

Jobs and Money

Without coral reefs or beautiful sea creatures, people would stop visiting some places in the world for their vacations. When people visit a place on vacation, it is called tourism. Tourism is good because people spend lots of money on vacation, and the places they visit get richer.

PLACES WITH CORAL REEFS HAVE LOTS OF VISITORS BECAUSE THEY ARE SO BEAUTIFUL.

Places like Australia and Fiji need tourism. A lot of their tourism comes from amazing things like coral reefs. Without tourism, lots of people could lose their jobs and have no money to look after themselves.

IT MIGHT SEEM SURPRISING, BUT MILLIONS OF JOBS DEPEND ON PLANKTON AND WOULD BE LOST WITHOUT THEM.

WORRIED DOCTORS AND SICK PEOPLE

MEDICAL CENTER

ATTENTION PATIENTS

Some of the medicines we use no longer work. Your doctor might not be able to treat some illnesses. We are very sorry.

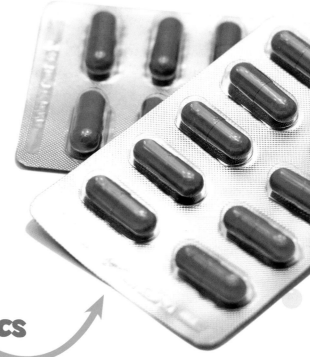

The Problem with Old Medicine

When someone has an **infection**, doctors give them a type of medicine called an antibiotic. Antibiotics are used to treat all sorts of things, like ear and eye infections. Antibiotics kill **bacteria**, but some bacteria are changing and can't be destroyed. Doctors and scientists think that our antibiotics won't work forever. This means we need to find new ways of making antibiotics.

Antibiotics

A New Hope

So far, a lot of medicines and antibiotics have come from plants on land. Around 120 medicines in the world today come straight from rain forest plants.

THE AMAZON RAIN FOREST IS THE BIGGEST RAIN FOREST. IT CONTAINS AROUND 40,000 SPECIES OF PLANTS.

However, scientists might find new types of medicine in the ocean. Corals, animals, and life found in ocean trenches might help us to create new antibiotics. Scientists think that the new medicines will be able to kill the new bacteria. However, without plankton, no life would survive in the ocean, which would mean that no new medicines could be found.

Ocean trenches can be up to 7 miles (11 km) deep. Sunlight does not reach the bottom of the trenches.

Ocean Trench

SO CLOSE TO A CURE

tweeter

Professor Tess Tube
@Bensonrules

⚙ 👤 FOLLOW

No! We were SO CLOSE to finding a cure! All we needed was a little longer to study the coral reefs... If anyone needs me, I'll be at home with a bucket of ice cream, feeling sad.
#ComeBackPlankton #AlgaeSavesLives
#MaybeIWillHaveTwoBuckets

223,958,022 Retweets   **824,223** Likes

  ❤

 Reply to @Bensonrules

Under the Sea

Scientists now think that the cures to all kinds of illnesses might be found in the ocean. Unlike on land, not many people have explored the ocean for medicine. Although these cures might not come from plankton, they will definitely come from creatures that need plankton to survive.

Humans have only explored 5% of the ocean.

16

Sea Sponges

Some illnesses, like **cancer**, can be very serious. Although there are ways to treat cancer, scientists are always looking for even better medicines. Some of these medicines have been found in sea sponges. Sea sponges are creatures that live throughout the ocean, and they contain **chemicals** that have already been used in cancer medicines. There may be even more useful chemicals to find.

What Do Sea Sponges Eat?

Sea sponges mostly eat algae or other microscopic plankton. They would not survive if the plankton disappeared, and we would not find some cancer medicines if the sea sponges did not survive.

Some sea sponges measure less than 1 inch (2.5 cm), while others can be more than 10 feet (3 m) wide.

Sea Sponge

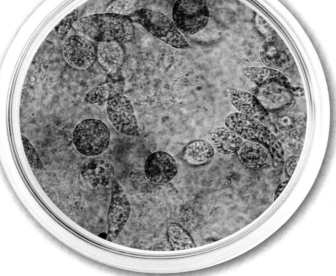

SEA SPONGES CAN GROW BACK PIECES OF THEMSELVES THAT HAVE BROKEN OFF.

EXTREME WEATHER

Your Local Weather
Friday, April 23, 2024

9:41   100%

Heavy Snow
19°

Sat		32°	21°
Sun		64°	48°
Mon		50°	41°
Tue		75°	70°
Wed		68°	61°
Thu		61°	46°

Climate Change

Humans do a lot of things that aren't good for the **environment**. When we burn **fossil fuels** to make electricity or to fuel cars or planes, a gas called carbon dioxide is released into the air. Carbon dioxide causes more heat to be trapped on Earth, which can change the weather (or climate) all around the world. This is called climate change.

CLIMATE CHANGE CAN LEAD TO MORE EXTREME WEATHER IN SOME PARTS OF THE WORLD, SUCH AS HURRICANES AND FLOODS.

Carbon Underwater

A lot of carbon is stored in the oceans. This is because phytoplankton take in carbon, water, and sunlight and use these things to make energy. Dead plankton, and dead animals that have eaten plankton, sink to the bottom of the ocean. The carbon is stored in the ocean until it naturally rises.

When tiny bits of living things sink to the ocean floor, it is sometimes called marine snow.

THE WORLD'S PHYTOPLANKTON TAKE UP A LOT LESS ROOM THAN THE WORLD'S PLANTS. HOWEVER, PHYTOPLANKTON TAKE IN 40% OF THE CARBON.

There would be much more carbon in the air if it weren't for plankton. This means climate change would be much worse. There would be more hurricanes, floods, storms, and droughts. This would make life very hard for every animal on land, including humans.

Algae Under a Microscope

CLOUD
CONTROL

"LOOKING OUT OVER THE OCEANS, IT LOOKS LIKE IT IS GOING TO BE CLEAR TODAY, TOMORROW, THE DAY AFTER THAT, AND... WHY ARE THERE SO FEW CLOUDS OVER THE SEA NOW? THERE MUST BE SOMETHING MISSING FROM THE OCEAN. WHAT PLANTS OR ANIMALS IN THE OCEAN COULD BE THAT IMPORTANT?"

The Answer Is Always Plankton

Plankton help create clouds over the ocean. Clouds are made up of tiny droplets of water that stick to **particles**. When enough of these droplets get together, a cloud is formed.

Albedo

Albedo is the amount of sunlight that Earth reflects. Some things reflect a lot of sunlight, like fluffy white clouds, or the snowy North and South Poles. Other things don't reflect as much sunlight, like the oceans and forests.

The amount of sunlight reflected by an ocean cloud depends on how many particles and droplets it is made up of.

Cooling Down

Reflecting or blocking sunlight is a good thing because it keeps the planet cooler. A cooler planet means the climate probably won't change as much. This means that plankton are also helping keep the weather safe and normal by helping to create clouds.

ALTHOUGH PLANKTON HELP KEEP THE EARTH COOL, THEY CAN'T ALWAYS KEEP UP WITH WHAT HUMANS DO TO THE ENVIRONMENT.

THE EARTH
GETS OUT OF BREATH

"T-THIS IS ... THE NEWS. OUR ... OUR TOP STORY TONIGHT IS ... SORRY, I'M A BIT OUT OF BREATH. NO ... REALLY, THAT IS THE TOP STORY.
SINCE ... THE PLANKTON DISAPPEARED, THERE ... ISN'T MUCH ... AIR THAT WE CAN BREATHE. OK ... IT IS TIME FOR THE WEATHER ... I'M GOING TO GO AND LIE DOWN."

BREAKING NEWS
BREAKING NEWS
LIVE NEWS
WHERE'S THE AIR?
GLOBAL OXYGEN OUTAGE

What Do You Need to Survive?

There are a few things that every human needs in order to survive. Everyone needs food, sleep, water, and oxygen. Oxygen is all around us in the air that we breathe. But where does it come from?

The Carbon Cycle

Oxygen is released by plants and plankton. Humans and animals breathe oxygen in and breathe out carbon dioxide. Plants and plankton take in carbon dioxide, as well as sunlight and water, to give them the energy that they need to survive. Then it happens all over again. This is called the carbon cycle.

The Carbon Cycle

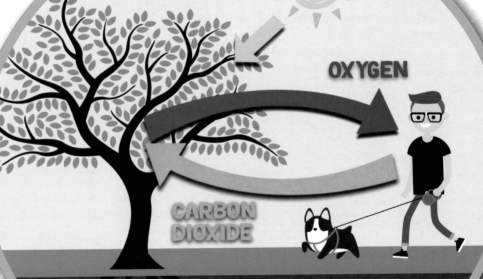

Plankton create half of the oxygen that we breathe.

The carbon cycle shows how different forms of life work together. Animals and plants need each other to survive. The oxygen that plankton release is especially important for the animals in the sea, but it affects humans, too.

A WORLD WITH TOO MUCH PLANKTON

BREAKING NEWS

STAY AWAY FROM RIVERS, LAKES, AND OCEANS.

A huge number of plankton have appeared from nowhere! These areas of water are now quite dangerous. Do not eat anything that has recently come from the nearby oceans. A full story will be released soon.

SOME ALGAE BLOOMS CAN BE SEEN FROM SPACE.

Blooms can be green, yellow, or red.

The Dark Side of Plankton

When lots of new algae appear, it is called a bloom. In a bloom there can be hundreds or even thousands of algae **cells** in every milliliter of water. However, if there is too much plankton, this can be harmful to everything in the water.

The Red Tide

Red tides are out-of-control blooms of certain types of plankton. Some red tides can be harmful. The plankton may release **toxins,** which are dangerous to the other animals in the water. If people catch and eat animals that have eaten toxins, it is dangerous for the people, too. It can also be difficult to breathe in the air around the bloom.

When lots of algae die and **rot**, it uses up a lot of oxygen in the water. This is bad for the other animals, as they might not have enough oxygen to live.

RED TIDES ARE ALSO CALLED HARMFUL ALGAL BLOOMS (HABS).

The same type of plankton that causes red tides can also glow in the dark sometimes.

THREATS
TO PLANKTON

Northern Hemisphere

A world without plankton looks quite scary. While they do still exist in today's world, they are in danger.

After studying plankton, scientists have found that there is less plankton in all of the oceans than there was 20 years ago. This is especially true in the Northern Hemisphere. There are many reasons why there is less plankton around the world today.

A WARMER WORLD IS CAUSED BY HOW HUMANS LIVE.

Climate Change

As the world gets warmer, scientists think this might be affecting plankton. Warmer water in the ocean doesn't mix with the colder water underneath, which contains **nutrients**. This makes it harder for plankton to grow and survive.

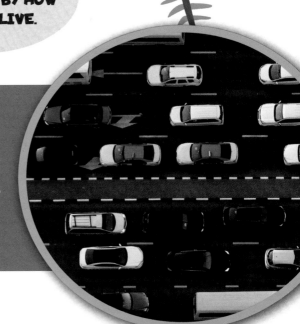

Warmer waters might force plankton to be closer to the North and South Poles. This is because the temperature would be lower in these areas, and they would find it easier to survive.

IF PLANKTON MOVED AROUND THE WORLD, IT WOULD ALSO CHANGE WHERE OTHER ANIMALS WOULD LIVE.

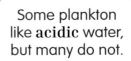

Some plankton like **acidic** water, but many do not.

Acid Ocean

Because humans are creating so much carbon dioxide, the ocean is taking in more and more carbon. This makes the water more acidic. Plankton need to have the water just right – if the water was too acidic, many plankton would die out.

Plastic

Many people know that plastic in the ocean can be dangerous for animals. Sea turtles swallow plastic bags because they think they are jellyfish, and this is very harmful. However, plankton can also swallow very tiny bits of plastic, which can kill them.

MANY ANIMALS THINK THE PLASTIC IS FOOD.

There are around 51 trillion particles of plastic in oceans all over the world.

Humans dump a lot of trash in the sea, including plastic. If this continues, it may be very harmful to ocean life. It is important that people recycle plastic and companies cut down on the amount of plastic that they use.

MOST PLASTIC DOESN'T BREAK DOWN FOR HUNDREDS OF YEARS.

Do Humans Cause Red Tides?

Nobody is exactly sure what causes red tides. Extreme weather may be one cause, while wind and water currents could be another. Many people think that humans sometimes cause them, too. They think this happens when extra nutrients flow into the water from lawns and farmland.

Chinese Farmland

Is There One Reason?

Plankton have a lot of things to deal with. There probably isn't one single reason why plankton are disappearing. Rather, it is probably lots of reasons all added up. However, there are things being done to save plankton and the rest of the environment.

Orange Nettle Jellyfish

SAVING
THE PLANKTON

Although climate change is still a problem, humans have done many good things for the environment. For example, the Paris Climate Agreement is an agreement between countries to release less carbon dioxide into the air.

Things like solar panels and wind turbines create electricity in a way that is friendly to the environment. This is called green energy, and it is more popular than ever.

What Can You Do to Help?

- Recycle! Ask an adult to help you find out what can be recycled.

- To save electricity, turn off things like lights and televisions when you are not using them. You could also ask your parents if they are using energy-saving light bulbs.

- Talk about plankton! Tell everyone that they are one of the most important tiny things in the world.

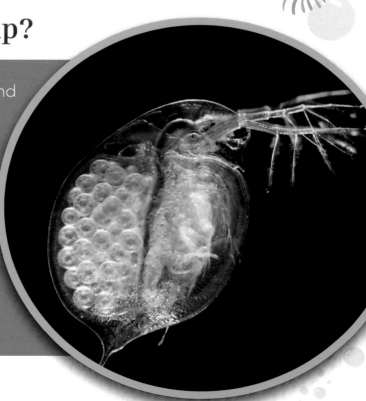

GLOSSARY

acidic	contains a chemical substance that causes damage to the natural environment
bacteria	microscopic living things that can cause diseases
baleen plates	the part of a whale's mouth that is used for filtering
cancer	a serious disease caused by the uncontrolled dividing of cells
cells	the basic units that make up all living things
chemicals	substances that materials are made from
currents	steady flows of water in one direction
economically	in a way that relates to the system by which goods and services are made, bought, and sold in a place, called the economy
environment	the natural world
fossil fuels	fuels, such as coal, oil, and gas, that formed millions of years ago from the remains of animals and plants
infection	an illness caused by germs getting into the body
microscope	an instrument used by scientists to see very small things
nutrients	natural substances that plants and animals need to grow and stay healthy
particles	extremely small pieces of a substance
rot	spoil and break down
toxins	poisonous substances

INDEX

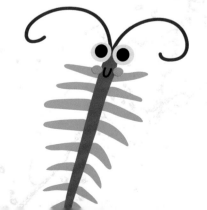